O9-ABE-372

Daily Discoveries

for October

Thematic Learning Activities for
EVERY DAY

Written by Elizabeth Cole Midgley

Illustrated by Jennette Guymon-King

Teaching & Learning Company

1204 Buchanan St., P.O. Box 10
Carthage, IL 62321-0010

J 371.33
MID

This book belongs to

_____

Cover art by Jennette Guymon-King

Copyright © 2005, Teaching & Learning Company

ISBN No. 1-57310-454-X

Printing No. 987654321

Teaching & Learning Company
1204 Buchanan St., P.O. Box 10
Carthage, IL 62321-0010

The purchase of this book entitles teachers to make copies for use in their individual classrooms, only. This book, or any part of it, may not be reproduced in any form for any other purposes without prior written permission from the Teaching & Learning Company. It is strictly prohibited to reproduce any part of this book for an entire school or school district, or for commercial resale.

All rights reserved. Printed in the United States of America.

Before offering any food to your students, make sure you are aware of any allergies or dietary restrictions your students may have.

At the time of publication every effort was made to insure the accuracy of the information included in this book. However, we cannot guarantee that agencies and organizations mentioned will continue to operate or maintain these current locations.

Table of Contents

Dear Teacher or Parent,

Due to the stimulus of a high-tech world, parents and teachers are often faced with the challenge of how to capture the attention of a child and create an atmosphere of meaningful learning opportunities. Often we search for new ways to meet this challenge and help young people transfer their knowledge, skills and experiences from one area to another. Subjects taught in isolation can leave a feeling of fragmentation. More and more educators are looking for ways to be able to integrate curriculum so that their students can fully understand how things relate to each other.

The Daily Discoveries series has been developed to that end. Quite naturally, many of the themes and ideas in this October book focus on the month's big celebration, Halloween. For many, this holiday has long since left its origins and has been taken over by children as one of the best excuses all year to dress up, act silly and eat candy! It is in this spirit that the Halloween activities in this book are offered. For those who eschew the holiday, most of the ideas can readily be used without reference to Halloween.

In this series, each day has been researched around the history of a specific individual or event and has been developed into a celebration or theme with integrated curriculum areas. In this approach to learning, students draw from their own experience and understanding of things to a level of processing new information and skills. Each day students can be involved in creating a web or semantic map with what they already know and then add additional information as the day progresses.

The Daily Discoveries series is an almanac-of-sorts, 12 books (one for each month) that present a thematically based curriculum for grades K-6. The series contains hundreds and hundreds of resources and ideas that can be a natural springboard to learning. These ideas have been used in the classroom and at home and are fun as well as educationally sound. The activities have been endorsed by professors, teachers, parents and, best of all, by children themselves.

The Daily Discoveries series can be used in the following ways for school or home:
- to develop new skills and reinforce previous learning
- to create a sense of fun and celebration in the every day
- tutoring resources
- enrichment activities that can be used as time allows
- family fun activities

Sincerely,

Elizabeth

Elizabeth Cole Midgley

TLC10454 Copyright © Teaching & Learning Company, Carthage, IL 62321-0010

Fitness Day

October 1

Setting the Stage
- Display pictures of people involved in fitness training activities around related literature.

- Display student work around pictures of people exercising with the caption, "Physically FIT, Mentally FIT!"

- Construct a semantic web around facts your students already know (or want to know) about fitness to help you structure your day's activities.

- Please be aware of any physical restrictions or limitations any of your students may have before engaging in any energetic activity.

Historical Background
World records were set by both Roger Maris (breaking Babe Ruth's baseball home run record) and Steve McKinney (breaking snow skier speed records) on this day in 1961 and 1978. Do you think these men believed in the importance of being physically fit?

Literary Exploration
Albert the Running Bear's Exercise Book by Barbara Isenberg and Marjorie Jaffe
Arnold's Fitness for Kid's Ages Birth to 5: A Guide to Health, Exercise and Nutrition by Arnold Schwarzenegger
Arnold's Fitness for Kid's Ages 6-10: A Guide to Health, Exercise and Nutrition by Arnold Schwarzenegger
Bodyworks: The Kid's Guide to Food and Fitness by Carol Bershad
Exercise and Fitness by Brian R. Ward
Fun with Fitness by A. Roberts

TLC10454 Copyright © Teaching & Learning Company, Carthage, IL 62321-0010

Language Experience
- Encourage your students to see how many words they can come up with that rhyme with *fit*.

Fitness

Writing Experience
- Ask students to write about how they feel when they are physically fit and can do what they want to do (hiking, pushups, etc.) without tiring. See reproducible on page 10.

How I feel when I am fit, fit, fit!

Name: _____

Fitness

Math Experience
- Students can begin graphing their fitness skills on a chart to keep track of their progress. For example, as they increase their ability to do more sit-ups, the chart will reflect that growth.

Fitness

TLC10454 Copyright © Teaching & Learning Company, Carthage, IL 62321-001

Science/Health Experience

• Today is a great chance to begin a health unit on lifetime fitness skills (nutrition and general health, personal safety, exercise, adequate rest).

Social Studies Experience

• Begin a physical fitness program entitled "Fitness Across America!" Display a map of the United States, pointing out the area from the Pacific Coast to the Atlantic Coast. Challenge students to get physically fit by running from one coast to the other by the end of the school year. Children may wish to use a pedometer to keep track of their actual "mileage," or you may wish to award "mile points" for various classroom activities or accomplishments. Celebrate at the end of the year (or when you reach the Atlantic) with a party, serving healthy snacks.

Fitness

Fitness

Fitness

Music/Dramatic Experience

• Let students play Fitness Charades! They pantomime various fitness skills for others to guess (jumping jacks, pull-ups, etc).

Physical/Sensory Experience

• Get students involved in fitness activities to increase cardiovascular endurance, strength and flexibility. Let them decide which activities they might like to do today such as running, jump roping, shooting baskets or dancing to favorite music.

TLC10454 Copyright © Teaching & Learning Company, Carthage, IL 62321-0010

Arts/Crafts Experience

• Let students draw pictures of fitness activities: exercise, eating nutritiously, adequate rest and avoiding harmful substances. Have them fold their art paper into fourths, then label each drawing with a fitness idea or tip.

Extension Activities

• Invite a fitness expert from a local gym or health club to come and talk about general fitness.

Values Education Experience

• Stress the importance and value of having a strong body and mind to help us achieve the things we want to do in life.

Follow-Up/Homework Idea

• Encourage students to walk or ride a bike, whenever possible, instead of asking Mom to drive them everywhere, to eat a healthy snack when they go home today and to go outside and get some fresh air instead of turning on the TV and grabbing a bag of potato chips. Remind them that having a healthy body is a choice they make every day.

How I feel when I am fit, fit, fit!

Name: _____

TLC10454 Copyright © Teaching & Learning Company, Carthage, IL 62321-0010

Gandhi's Birthday

October 2

Setting the Stage
• Display pictures of Gandhi around related literature to gather interest in the day's emphasis.

Historical Background
Known as the "Father of India," Mahatma Gandhi was born on this day in 1869. His method of nonviolent resistance helped India achieve independence and brought him international recognition.

Literary Exploration
Gandhi by Brenda Clarke
Gandhi by Leonard Everett
Gandhi by Doris Faber
Gandhi by Nigel Hunter
Gandhi, Fighter Without a Sword by Eaton
Mahatma Gandhi by Caroline Lazo
Mahatma Gandhi: Champion of Human Rights by Beverley Birch
Mahatma Gandhi: The Man Who Freed India by Michael Nicholson
Peaceful Fighter, Gandhi by Elizabeth Rider Montgomery

Language Experience
• Before telling students that Gandhi was given the name Mahatma by his people, meaning "great soul," let them try to figure out his name by playing the Clothesline Game. Play Hangman, hanging clothes on the line rather than people.

Writing Experience

• Gandhi made a real difference in the lives of those around him as they watched the quiet, but powerful, way his ideas affected the course of his life. Encourage your students to write about what they would like to do to make a difference in the lives of others. See reproducible on page 13.

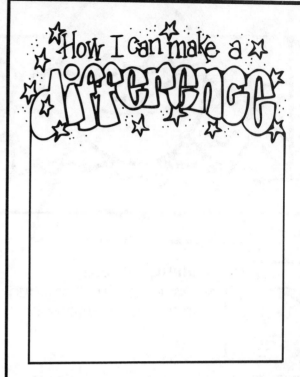

How I can make a difference

Name:_____

Social Studies Experience

• Let students research the life and contributions of Gandhi.

• Study the life and culture of India.

Music/Dramatic Experience

• Gandhi was known for reform through nonviolent, peaceful demonstrations. Allow students to role-play situations in which they practice change through nonviolence. (Example: a bully picking a fight with another student)

Values Education Experience

• Discuss what Gandhi may have meant when he said, "There is more to life than increasing its speed."

Follow-Up/Homework Idea

• Challenge students to look for ways to resolve problems and make changes in peaceful, non-violent ways.

TLC10454 Copyright © Teaching & Learning Company, Carthage, IL 62321-0010

How I Can make a difference

Name: _____

TLC10454 Copyright © Teaching & Learning Company, Carthage, IL 62321-0010

Octoberfest Day

October 3
(varies)

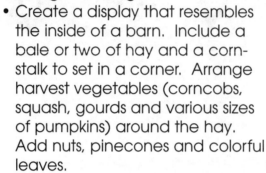

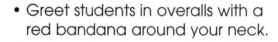

Setting the Stage

• Create a display that resembles the inside of a barn. Include a bale or two of hay and a corn-stalk to set in a corner. Arrange harvest vegetables (corncobs, squash, gourds and various sizes of pumpkins) around the hay. Add nuts, pinecones and colorful leaves.

• Greet students in overalls with a red bandana around your neck.

Historical Background

The first October festival was held in 1810 to celebrate the wedding of Germany's King Ludwig and his new queen, Theresa. Germany celebrates "Oktoberfest" in late September and early October with parades, harvest displays and all kinds of food.

TLC10454 Copyright © Teaching & Learning Company, Carthage, IL 62321-0010

Literary Exploration

Barn Dance! by Bill Martin, Jr., with illustrations by Ted Rand. An after-hours animal hoedown is described in rollicking text and vibrant illustrations. The rhythm is catching, your students may want to create some verses of their own.

Language Experience

• How many new words can students make using the letters in *Octoberfest*?

Social Studies Experience

• Ancient Druids held a festival to celebrate the end of summer and the fall harvest. Today, countries around the world still celebrate this time of year, giving thanks for another year of a successful harvest with dancing, food and games. Let interested students research harvest festivals around the world and share this information with the rest of the class.

Music/Dramatic Experience

• Sing the classic children's song, "The Farmer in the Dell."

Physical/Sensory Experience

• Play the Barnyard Animal Game! Whisper to individual students the name of a barnyard animal. Instead of giving the same one over and over, use three different animals. Students try to locate others who have been given the same animal. They can do this only by making the sound of their animal. The first group to locate all their fellow animals wins.

Arts/Crafts Experience

• Let students shape a cornucopia with harvest vegetables from modeling clay.

• Students can draw a harvest mosaic in the shape of a corncob or cornucopia, then glue popcorn kernels, seeds or beans inside the shape.

Extension Activities

• Host a Barnyard Bash! Borrow square dance music from a local library so students can have a "barn dance." Younger students might enjoy putting hay or straw in a small wagon and going for a "hay ride." Serve dough-nuts or pumpkin bread and apple cider.

16

Sneakers and Stuff Day

October 4

Setting the Stage

- "Step" into a fun day today with a theme about shoes! Display all kinds of shoes around related literature to get your students excited about a day that can go unde-"feet"-ed in fun and interest!

- Construct a semantic web with facts students know (or want to know) about shoes to help plan the rest of the day.

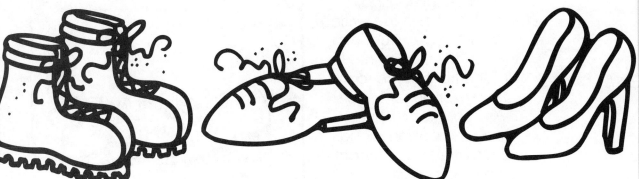

Literary Exploration

The Adventures of Albert the Running Bear by Barbara Isenberg and Susan Wolf
Dogs Don't Wear Sneakers by Laura Joffee Numeroff
Hector's New Sneakers by A. Vesey
Sneakers: The Shoes We Choose! by Robert Young
What if the Shark Wears Tennis Shoes? by Winifred Morris

Language Experience

• Let students brainstorm words that rhyme with *shoes.*

Writing Experience

• Have students each take off a shoe and place it on their desk. They should observe their shoes carefully noting every detail before writing about them. Have them write a paper about how the shoe looks (and smells). When the writing period is over, students place their shoes in a line at the front of the room. They exchange papers with each other and read the papers aloud. Everyone tries to locate the shoe based on the description.

If my **tennis shoes** talked they would say......

Name: _____

• Challenge students to write about what their tennis shoes might say if they could talk. See reproducible on page 20.

Social Studies Experience

• Provide students with a pattern of a shoe from a specific era of history. Have them write about a person in history they have admired who might have worn the shoe. (Example: moccasin—Daniel Boone) Students should include in their writing how they would like to follow "in the footsteps" of that person.

TLC10454 Copyright © Teaching & Learning Company, Carthage, IL 62321-0010

Physical/Sensory Experience

- Have a shoe relay. Divide students into relay teams. Each runner runs to a designated area, takes off one shoe, places it in a pile and runs back so the next person can do the same. The relay teams will run four times (two for taking off their shoes and two for putting on their shoes). The first team to have both shoes back on and sitting down in their line, wins.

Arts/Crafts Experience

- Let students invent and design new kinds of tennis shoes, such as a tennis shoe that plays soothing music while you walk and upbeat music when you run.

Extension Activities

- Invite a local high school track star to come and talk about his or her experience with running and the importance of good sneakers or running shoes to support your feet.

- Perhaps your class can sponsor a shoe drive to help provide shoes for the needy in a local homeless shelter.

Values Education Experience

- Discuss what it means to "fill another's shoes."

Follow-Up/Homework Idea

- Ask students to go home and organize the shoes in their closet according to color or function.

If my tennis shoes talked they would say......

Name: _____

TLC10454 Copyright © Teaching & Learning Company, Carthage, IL 62321-0010

Relay Rumpus Day

October 5

Setting the Stage
• Construct a semantic web with words your students think of when you say, "relay."

Literary Exploration
Huff and Puff's Hat Relay by Jean Warren

Language Experience
• Let students name all the relays they can remember (basketball dribble, wheelbarrow, Hula Hoop, jump rope, backwards races, crabwalk), then list them in alphabetical order.

Writing Experience
• Divide class into relays to come up with descriptive words about a particular noun such as *toads*. Tally the points and see which team has thought of the most descriptive words. This game can be played with almost any word that needs reinforcing.

Math Experience
- Create a relay out of your current math topic (addition, subtraction, place value, multiplication).

Physical/Sensory Experience
- Students love relays that test their speed, agility, coordination and balance. Here are some relay favorites:

Tunnel Relay
Divide the class into teams and line up on one end of the gym. The leader crawls through the legs of the others in his line. The second person begins to crawl through as soon as the first crawler has cleared the first person in the tunnel. This continues until a team reaches the end of the gym.

Beanbag Relay
Divide into relay teams. At the signal, team members balance a beanbag on their heads to a designated area, then back to the starting line.

TLC10454 Copyright © Teaching & Learning Company, Carthage, IL 62321-0010

Over-Under Relay

Divide into two relay teams, each forming a line. Choose a captain for each team. The captain begins by passing a ball over his head to the next person who passes it under his legs. They continue this over, under, over, under to the end of the line. The last person runs to the front of the line and becomes the new captain, repeating the pattern. The team to reach the other side of the gym first wins.

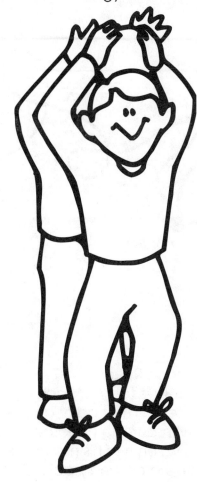

Bow-Legged Relay

Divide students into teams. Have them take turns hopping to a designated area and back with a ball between their knees. The team that finishes first wins.

Relay Rumpus

Relay Rumpus

Relay Rumpus

Balloon Relay

Divide students into teams. Give each team an inflated balloon and a piece of cardboard (or thick construction paper). The first person on each team fans the balloon with the cardboard to a designated area and back. Then the next person in line repeats the same procedure. The team that finishes and sits down first wins.

Egg on a Spoon Relay

Divide into relays teams. Each person on the team must carry a plastic spoon with an egg (or large marshmallow) on it in his mouth to a designated area and back. The tricky part is handing the egg (or marshmallow) to the next person (moving it from one person's spoon to the other's without using hands).

TLC10454 Copyright © Teaching & Learning Company, Carthage, IL 62321-0010

National Children's Day

October 6
(varies)

Setting the Stage

• Tell students they are all kings today and will get to have a voice in what happens in class, choosing their favorite things to do in each curriculum area.

• Construct a semantic map with words your students think of when you say, "children."

Historical Background

On October 11, 1991, President George H.W. Bush signed a proclamation designating the second Sunday in October as National Children's Day. In the text, President Bush urged ". . . all Americans to reflect upon the importance of stable, loving families to our children and to our nation." (Subsequent annual Presidential Proclamations have named a specific date for the holiday—most often in early October.)

Literary Exploration

"Children, Children Everywhere" Poem by Jack Prelutsky from *The Random House Book of Poetry*.
Children Just Like Me by Bamabus and Anabel Kindersley (in association with *Unicef*)
I Am Not a Short Adult: Getting Good at Being a Kid by Marilyn Burns

Language Experience

• Let students decide which reading or language area they would like to review.

Writing Experience

• Have students write a paper about the best or the hardest thing about being a kid.

Math Experience

• Personalize today's math lesson: Use students' names in story problems; have students figure out the class averages for height, shoe size, arm length, etc.; graph eye or hair color, favorite food (or pet, song, movie, sport, hero, etc.); play "telephone" with a simple equation and award a small prize for the correct answer.

Science/Health Experience

• What favorite topic in science and health would students like to discuss or what experiment have they always wanted to perform?

Social Studies Experience

• What historical event or person would students like to know more about? Try to obtain a copy of *We Were There, Too* by Phillip Hoose. It highlights contributions of young people to events in American history from Columbus' voyage to the present.

Music/Dramatic Experience

• Let students nominate classmates for a SuperKid Award! Each student can only be nominated once. Nominators must tell why their nominees should be chosen as the Class SUPERKID! No need to vote; this is just a chance for students to sing the praises of one another. Make sure every student nominates someone so no one is left out. Give everyone an award. See award patterns on page 28.

TLC10454 Copyright © Teaching & Learning Company, Carthage, IL 62321-001

Physical/Sensory Experience

• What favorite indoor or outdoor game would students like to play today?

Arts/Crafts Experience

• Vote on a favorite art medium the class would like to work with today (chalk pastels, watercolor, clay, sketching).

• Students can make their own "King (Queen) Kid" crowns, decorating them with glitter, paint, sequins or whatever is available.

Values Education Experience

• Discuss the importance of children in the world. Children provide fresh excitement, enthusiasm and ideas!

Follow-Up/Homework Idea

• Encourage students to enjoy this time in their lives!

I'm SUPER because...

I'm SUPER because...

I'm a Superkid

I'm a Superkid

TLC10454 Copyright © Teaching & Learning Company, Carthage, IL 62321-001

One of a Kind Day

October 7

One of
a Kind

One of
a Kind

One of
a Kind

Setting the Stage

- Display a mirror (that can be left up for a while) in an area on your students' eye level. Above it print the caption: "You are attractive and capable!"

Literary Exploration

Brave Irene by William Steig
Charlie the Caterpillar by Dom Deluise
Dandelion by Don Freeman
Every Kid's Guide to Being Special by Joy Berry
I Like Me by Nancy Carlson
I Like to Be Me by Barbara Bel Geddes
I'm Terrific! by Marjorie Weinman Shrmat
I Really Like Myself by Dorothy Kottler
Just Me by Marie Hall Ets
Leo, the Late Bloomer by Robert Krauss
A Mighty, Muddy Lesson by Jack Girst
Shy Charles by Rosemary Wells
Someday by Charlotte Zolotow
There Is Only One Me by Julie Gibbons
To Be Me by Barbara Shook Hazen
Who's That in the Mirror? by Polly Berends
Why Am I Different? by Norma Simon
You Look Ridiculous by Bernard Most

Language Experience

• Explain to students that you value their opinions and ideas. Encourage them to share their ideas and suggestions by putting them in a suggestion box or notebook that can be kept up all year.

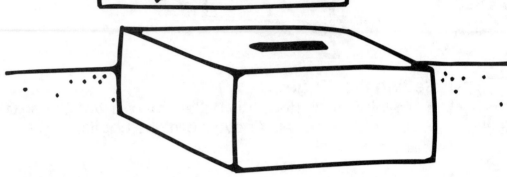

Writing Experience

• Let students brainstorm words that they feel best describe themselves. Have them use the words in a writing assignment about how they see themselves and how they think others see them. See reproducible on page 34.

• Have students write cinquains about themselves, following this pattern:

First line: title
Second line: two adjectives
Third line: three verbs
Fourth line: a simile
Fifth line: synonym for title

Student Example:

Matthew
Smart, funny
Helping, laughing, reading
The cat's meow
Matt

Words that describe ME!

Name: _____

TLC10454 Copyright © Teaching & Learning Company, Carthage, IL 62321-001

Math Experience

• Let students measure the circumference of each other's heads or the length of each other's arms, legs and feet to show how we are different even at the same age. This information can be added to a class graph.

Science/Health Experience

• Today is a perfect day to begin an emotional health unit on self-concept. Explain that you are going to introduce someone to them who is very attractive, capable and interesting. Explain that even with all the millions of people on Earth, there is no one like this person and never will be. Elaborate as you feel necessary, then finally introduce the person. Bring out a full-length mirror and have students look into it. This will provide a springboard for further discussion and activities. Give each student a mirror (made of construction paper with aluminum foil for the glass) labeled: *I Am Special!* See reproducible on page 35.

I AM Special

Glue 4"x5"
tinfoil here.

There's no one on Earth like me!

One of
a Kind

One of
a Kind

One of
a Kind

Social Studies Experience

• Encourage students to share where their ancestors came from. Let students locate their families' places of origin on a world map. Students can decorate their family name or make a coat of arms and attach it to a piece of yarn or string to place near the location on the map.

Music/Dramatic Experience

• Sing "Feelin' Good About Myself" by Jacquelyn Reinach and Carmino Ravosa.

• Borrow Cathy Fink's sound recording of "Nobody Else Like Me" from your local library.

Physical/Sensory Experience

• Let students brag about other students. Give each one a long piece of yarn to wind (loosely) around a hand. At each loop or turn, a student can sing the praises or (brag about another student) while they are unwinding the yarn. They need to keep talking as long as there is yarn to be unwound. For a variation, have cards labeled *Me* or *You*, stacked facedown. Students pair up. When one picks a "Me" card, he says nice things about himself. When he picks a "You" card, he says nice things about his partner. See patterns on page 36.

TLC10454 Copyright © Teaching & Learning Company, Carthage, IL 62321-0010

Arts/Crafts Experience

• Let students each make a Profile Montage. Trace student profiles on black construction paper as they stand very still in front of the light of an overhead or slide projector. They can then add magazine cutouts or hand-drawn illustrations of things that typify their personalities or interests.

• Students can make life-sized self-portraits by drawing their facial features on paper plates, adding colored yarn for hair, wiggly eyes (found in craft stores), etc. They can cut body parts such as arms and legs from construction paper and add them to a paper torso. Each student can draw on clothing, then write on the self-portrait a description of himself or herself.

Follow-Up/Homework Idea

• Provide each student with a baby food jar containing m & m's™, jelly beans or other colored candies. Explain that we are all different (like the different colors of candies). Our differences are exciting and interesting. How boring life would be if we just ate one color of candy all the time. How boring if we were all just the same! As we get to know different people, we add to the "flavor" of our lives. Students could keep their jars of candy by their beds. When they wake up each morning, they should think about meeting at least one new person and finding out what makes that person unique. Each day as they do this, they can eat another color of candy to represent how they are expanding their circle of special people!

Words that describe ME!!

Name: _____

TLC10454 Copyright © Teaching & Learning Company, Carthage, IL 62321-001

I AM Special

Glue 4"x5"
tinfoil here.

There's no one on Earth like me!

TLC10454 Copyright © Teaching & Learning Company, Carthage, IL 62321-0010

36

TLC10454 Copyright © Teaching & Learning Company, Carthage, IL 62321-0010

Fire Prevention Day

October 8

Fire
Prevention

Fire
Prevention

Fire
Prevention

Setting the Stage

- Greet students wearing a plastic fire-fighter hat (found in novelty stores) and a plastic raincoat. Leave a trail of a garden hose leading into your classroom where they will find a display of fire prevention related literature.

- Construct a semantic web with facts students know (or would like to know) about fire prevention to help you structure the day's activities.

Historical Background

On this day in 1871 two horrendous fires claimed the lives of many, many people. A forest fire killed almost 1200 people in Peshtigo, Wisconsin, and the infamous "Great Chicago Fire" killed 250 people, destroying most of the city.

Literary Exploration

Fire Engines by Anne Rockwell
I Can Be a Fire Fighter by Rebecca Hankin
Number 9: The Little Fire Engine by Wallace Wadsworth
Safety First: Fire by Cynthia Klingel
The Little Fire Engine by Lois Lenski
The Little Fireman by Margaret Wise Brown
The Story of the Triangle Factory Fire by Zachary Kent
There'll Be a Hot Time in the Old Town Tonight by Robert Quackenbush
With Fire by Kyle Carter

Language Experience

• Challenge students to think of words that rhyme with *fire*.

Writing Experience

• Let students write safety rules for fire prevention. See reproducible on page 41.

• Students can write and obtain more information about fire prevention from:
National Fire Protection Association
470 Atlantic Ave.
Boston, MA 02210

• Teacher resources are available from www.smokeybear.com,
www.usfa.fema.gov/kids/parents-teachers/

TLC10454 Copyright © Teaching & Learning Company, Carthage, IL 62321-0010

Math Experience

• Draw a ladder (such as one used in fires) on the board. Use it to review math sequencing such as counting by ones, fives, tens, hundreds or other numbers.

Science/Health Experience

• Today is a great day to begin a health and safety unit on fire prevention.

Social Studies Experience

• Review mapping skills by letting students make a map of the classroom or their bedrooms, showing two escape routes in case of fire.

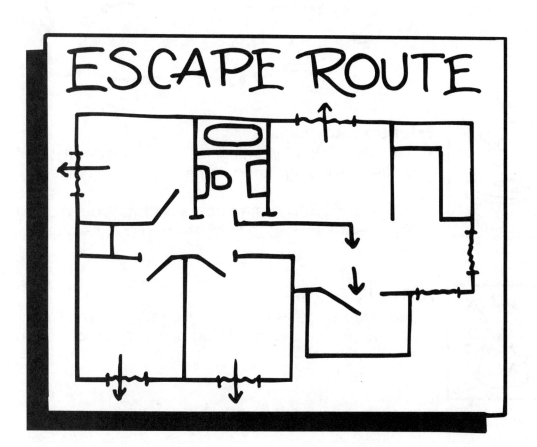

Music/Dramatic Experience
• Give students a chance to role-play what to do in fire situations, such as when clothes catch on fire or a person smells smoke behind a bedroom door.

Physical/Sensory Experience
• After discussing how to properly evacuate a building, have a fire drill.

Extension Activities
• Visit a fire station for a class field trip. Get permission for a tour of the facilities, including fire equipment and fire engines.

• Invite a local firefighter to come and visit your class to talk about what he or she does to fight fires and give helpful hints for preventing fires.

Follow-Up/Homework Idea
• Challenge students to involve their families in a fire drill after discussing what to do first and practicing alternative escape routes to a family meeting place.

TLC10454 Copyright © Teaching & Learning Company, Carthage, IL 62321-0010

Rules for GORE Prevention

Name:_____

TLC10454 Copyright © Teaching & Learning Company, Carthage, IL 62321-0010

Time
for
Time

Time
for
Time

Time
for
Time

Time for Time Day

October 9

Setting the Stage

- Invite students to write or cut out the numbers one through twelve to make a clock face on an over-turned paper plate. Display the clocks on a bulletin board with the caption: "TIME to learn!" or "The best time is . . . NOW!"

Literary Exploration

Around the Clock with Harriet by Betsy Maestro
Time by Richard Allington
Time by Jenny Tyler
Time To by Bruce McMillan

Writing Experience

- Have students write with story starters such as "I think the best time for me is . . ." or "The best time of my life has been . . ." They may write their stories on the shape of a pocket watch. See reproducible on page 44.

Story Time

Name: _____

42

TLC10454 Copyright © Teaching & Learning Company, Carthage, IL 62321-0010

Math Experience

• This is a perfect day to begin (or review) a math unit on telling time.

• Students will enjoy a Telling Bee (instead of Spelling Bee). Divide them into groups to work together to answer questions about the time on a demonstration clock. If a team member answers incorrectly, the whole team is eliminated and sits down.

Physical/Sensory Experience

• Blindfold one student at a time and play Pin the Hands on the Clock (a variation of Pin the Tail on the Donkey). Use patterns on page 45.

Arts/Crafts Experience

• Let students make their own clocks or watches (with moveable hands) by providing them with a paper plate, a brad fastener and construction paper. Students make hour and minute hands from construction paper and attach them to the center of the paper plate with the brad. Students then add the numbers in sequential order around the face of the clock. See patterns for clock on page 45. See patterns for watch on page 46.

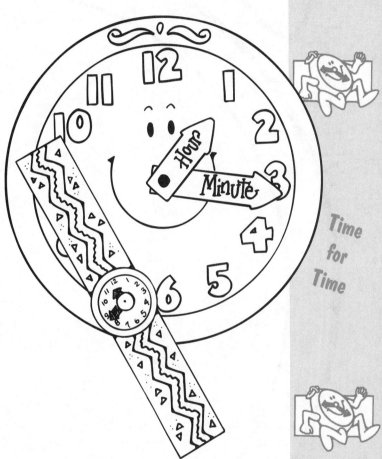

Values Education Experience

• This is a great opportunity to reinforce the value of making the most of whatever time we have to do and be our best.

Follow-Up/Homework Idea

• Encourage students to make sure they get home from school on time!

TLC10454 Copyright © Teaching & Learning Company, Carthage, IL 62321-0010

Name: _____

TLC10454 Copyright © Teaching & Learning Company, Carthage, IL 62321-0010

TLC10454 Copyright © Teaching & Learning Company, Carthage, IL 62321-0010

Backing

Glue backing on
(edges only) after
hands have been
attached by the
paper brad.

Backing

TLC10454 Copyright © Teaching & Learning Company, Carthage, IL 62321-0010

Amazing Alphabet Day

October 10

Setting the Stage

• Although you may think that this day is only for the youngest students, some activities such as alphabetizing are adaptable to any primary grades.

• Invite students ahead of time to bring something to share that begins or ends with a certain letter. These can be shared throughout the day as time permits.

Historical Background

Our current alphabet is based on the Greek alphabet, which was invented hundreds of years ago. Although it has undergone a few minimal changes, basically it is the same alphabet that was developed by the Greeks. There are, at present, about 65 different alphabets in use around the world (half of those are in India).

TLC10454 Copyright © Teaching & Learning Company, Carthage, IL 62321-0010

Literary Exploration

A B See! by Tana Hoban
A Is for Ark by Roger Duvoisin
A My Name Is Alice by Steven Kellogg
ABC by Brian Wildsmith
ABC Bunny by Wanda Gag
ABC Drive by Naomi Howland
Alphabatics by Suse MacDonald
Alphabears by Kathleen Hague
Alphabet Crafts by Kathy Darling
Alphabet Out Loud by Ruth Bragg
The Alphabet Tale by Jan Garten
Alphabet Town (series) by Janet McDonnell
Alphabet World by Barry Miller
Animal Alphabet by Bert Kitchen
Animalia by Graeme Base
Annie, Bea and Chi Chi Dolores by Donna Maurer
Annie's ABC by Annie Owen
Anno's Alphabet: An Adventure in Imagination by Mitsumasa Anno
Antler, Bear, Canoe: A Northwoods Alphabet Year by Betsy Bowen
Ape in a Cape: An Alphabet of Odd Animals by Fritz Eichenberg
An Around the World Alphabet by Jeanne Jeffares
The Bird Alphabet Book by Jerry Palotta
A Caribou Alphabet by Mary Beth Owens
Chicka Chicka Boom Boom by Bill Martin, Jr.
City Seen from A to Z by Rachel Isadora
Crictor by Tomi Ungerer
Demi's Find the Animal ABC by Demi
The Desert Alphabet Book by Jerry Palotta
The Dinosaur Alphabet Book by Jerry Palotta
Dr. Suess' ABC by Dr. Suess
Easy as Pie by Marcia and Michael Folsom
Eating the Alphabet: Fruits and Vegetables from A to Z by Lois Ehlert
Ed Emberley's ABC by Ed Emberley
The Extinct Alphabet Book by Jerry Palotta
The Flower Alphabet Book by Jerry Palotta
The Frog Alphabet Book by Jerry Palotta
From Acorn to Zoo by Satoshi Kitamura
The Furry Alphabet Book by Jerry Palotta
The Guinea Pig ABC by Kate Duke
The Handmade Alphabet by Laura Rankin
Handsigns: A Sign Language Alphabet by Kathleen Fain
Harold's ABC by Crockett Johnson
Hosie's Alphabet by Hosea

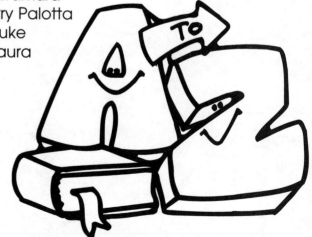

Amazing
Alphabet

Amazing
Alphabet

Amazing
Alphabet

TLC10454 Copyright © Teaching & Learning Company, Carthage, IL 62321-0010

Literary Exploration continued

The Icky Bug Alphabet Book by Jerry Palotta
I Spy: An Alphabet in Art by Lucy Micklethwait
I Unpacked My Grandmother's Trunk: A Picture Book Game by Susan Ramsay Hoguet
A Little Alphabet by Trina Schart Hyman
Marcel Marceau Alphabet Book by George Mendoza
The Ocean Alphabet Book by Jerry Palotta
Old Black Fly by Jim Aylesworth
On Market Street by Arnold Lobel
Q Is for Duck: An Alphabet Guessing Game by Mary Elting and Michael Folsom
Quentin Blake's ABC by Quentin Blake
The Underwater Alphabet Book by Jerry Palotta
Victoria's ABC Adventure by Cathy Warren
The Victory Garden Alphabet Book by Jerry Palotta
Wordworks: Why the Alphabet Is a Kid's Best Friend by Cathryn Berger
The Yucky Reptile Alphabet Book by Jerry Palotta
The Z Was Zapped by Chris Van Allsburg

Language Experience

- Let students have fun practicing their alphabetizing with alphabet-shaped pasta or Post Alphabits™ cereal. They can also cut letters from magazines (or from the patterns provided), place them in alphabetical order and paste them in a book or on art paper. See patterns on page 53.

Writing Experience

- Let older students try to write "A to Z" stories. These can be silly stories using a different letter of the alphabet, in order, in the sentences. (**A** **b**oy **c**ame **d**own the **e**scalator **f**requently **g**rabbing **h**old . . .) See reproducible on page 54.

- Another fun writing experience for older students is to write an "Alphabet Alliteration" patterned after Graeme Base's book, *Animalia*. Read the book together, then let them try to write their own.

Math Experience

- Play the Wordsworth Game. Assign every letter of the alphabet a monetary value (example: A = 1 cent, B = 2 cents). Each student must figure out how much his or her name is worth. Another option is to have them write a complete sentence under $1.00.

Science/Health Experience

- Share *ABC Alphabet Cookbook* by Dorothy Deers. Let students try to come up with a nutritious meal with the dishes in alphabetical order.

TLC10454 Copyright © Teaching & Learning Company, Carthage, IL 62321-0010

Social Studies Experience

• Experience a little world culture by reading Jeanne Jeffares' book *An Around the World Alphabet*.

Music/Dramatic Experience

• Let students pantomime the feelings found in *Marcel Marceau Alphabet Book* written by George Mendoza.

Physical/Sensory Experience

• Students will enjoy forming the letters of the alphabet from modeling clay.

• Let students have fun creating letters from their bodies. Other students may guess the letters. Two students may be needed for some letters.

Arts/Crafts Experience

• Your class might want to try some of the crafts in Kathy Darling's book called *Alphabet Crafts*.

• Have students write a few of their favorite letters of the alphabet, then create interesting people, animals or creatures out of them.

Extension Activities

• Make an "edible" alphabet. Students can shape refrigerated bread or breadstick dough (found in grocery stores) into individual letters of the alphabet. Then bake them for a tasty treat.

• Invite each of your students to bring a finger food beginning with a certain letter of the alphabet: C—carrot sticks, D—miniature dough-nuts. Make sure there's enough for everyone to have a taste of each food.

Follow-Up/Homework Idea

• Encourage students to check out one of the alphabet books from the list on pages 48 and 49 to read tonight.

TLC10454 Copyright © Teaching & Learning Company, Carthage, IL 62321-0010

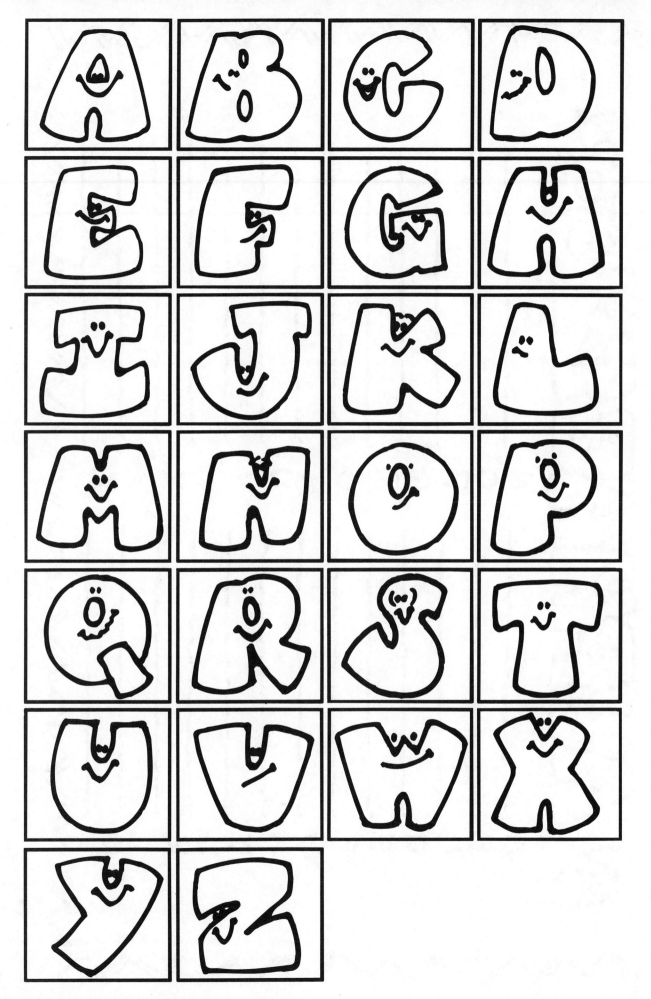

TLC10454 Copyright © Teaching & Learning Company, Carthage, IL 62321-0010

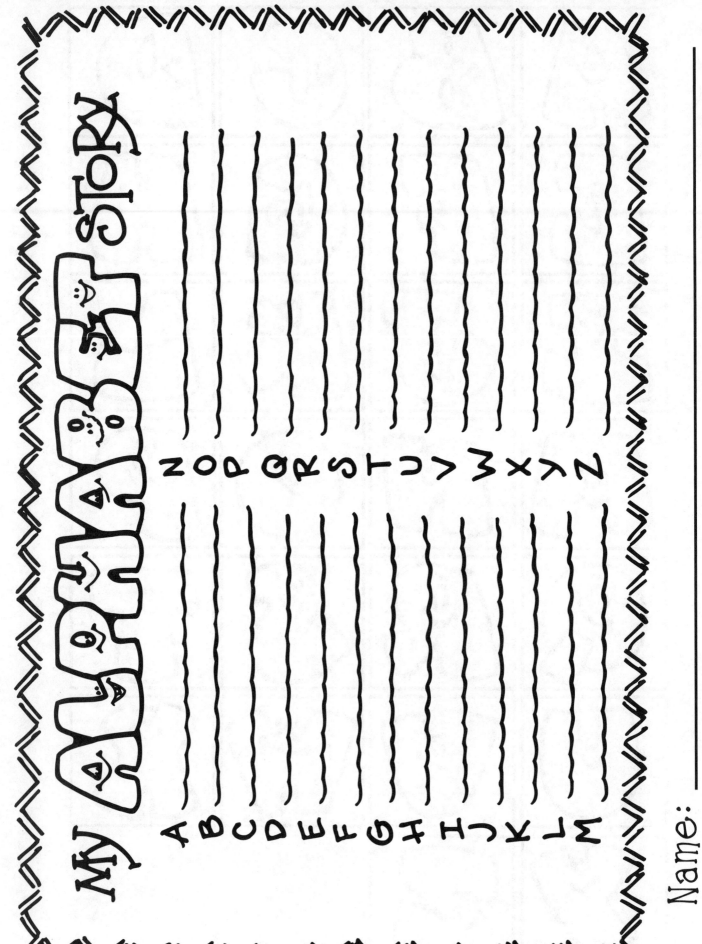

My ALPHABET Story

A B C D E F G H I J K L M

N O P Q R S T U V W X Y Z

TLC10454 Copyright © Teaching & Learning Company, Carthage, IL 62321-0010

Name: _____

Eleanor Roosevelt's Birthday

October 11

Setting the Stage
• Display pictures of Eleanor Roosevelt or of the Great Depression around related literature.

Historical Background
Eleanor Roosevelt, wife of President Franklin Delano Roosevelt, was born on this day in 1884. This first lady was a great humanitarian who spent much of her life helping those in less fortunate circumstances because of her concern for human rights.

Literary Exploration
Eleanor Roosevelt by Jane Goodsell
Eleanor Roosevelt by Charles Graves
Eleanor Roosevelt by Caroline Evensen Lazo
Eleanor Roosevelt by Karen McAuley
Eleanor Roosevelt by Rachel Toor
Eleanor Roosevelt by Jane Anderson Vercelli
Eleanor Roosevelt, Courageous Girl by Ann Weil
Eleanor Roosevelt: Fighter for Social Justice by Ann Weil
Eleanor Roosevelt, First Lady of the World by Doris Faber
Eleanor Roosevelt: A Life of Discovery by Russell Freedman
A Picture Book of Eleanor Roosevelt by David A. Adler
Young Eleanor Roosevelt by Francene Sabin

Language Experience

• How many words can your students make from the letters in *Eleanor Roosevelt*?

Writing Experience

• Eleanor overcame childhood shyness to speak up for issues and causes she believed in. Have students write about something that they feel strongly enough about to speak up for. See reproducible on page 58.

"I feel **STRONGLY** about . . ."

Name:_____

Social Studies Experience

• Study the period of time known as the Great Depression.

TLC10454 Copyright © Teaching & Learning Company, Carthage, IL 62321-0010

Values Education Experience

• Discuss what Eleanor Roosevelt may have meant when she said, "No one can make you feel inferior without your consent." See reproducible on page 59 for children to color and hang in their bedrooms.

No one can make you FEEL inferior without your CONSENT."
-Eleanor Roosevelt

Follow-Up/Homework Idea

• Encourage students to be advocates for fair treatment and human rights in the classroom, on the playground and in their neighborhoods.

"I feel STRONGLY about . . ."

Name: _____

TLC10454 Copyright © Teaching & Learning Company, Carthage, IL 62321-0010

"No one can make you FEEL inferior without your CONSENT."

-Eleanor Rosevelt

TLC10454 Copyright © Teaching & Learning Company, Carthage, IL 62321-0010

Christopher Columbus Day

October 12

Setting the Stage

- Display on a bulletin board the three ships Columbus sailed (the *Nina, Pinta* and *Santa Maria*) on a blue ocean background. Tear blue construction paper and layer it. Place the ships between the layers for a three-dimensional effect with the caption: "Columbus Had a Dream." Let students write on clouds about dreams they have. Mount the clouds above the ships. See ship pattern on page 69.

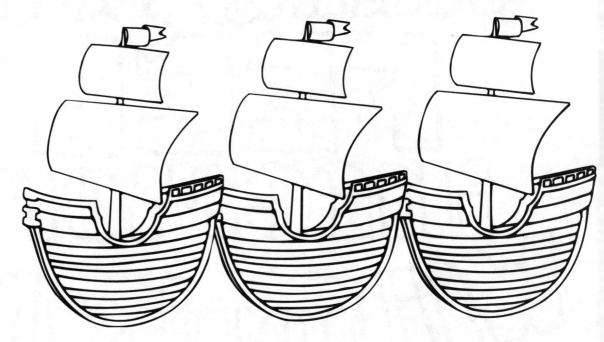

- Add book jacket covers around Columbus' ships with the caption, "Do some DISCOVERING of your own with books!"

- Construct a semantic map or web with the facts your students know about Christopher Columbus. Then, as a class, have them list things they'd like to discover about him today.

60

Historical Background

Christopher Columbus landed in the New World on this date in 1492. He thought he had found a route to India, so he called the people he found living there "Indians." The new land came to be known as "America."

Literary Exploration

All Pigs on Deck: Christopher Columbus' Second Marvelous Voyage by Laura Fischetto

A Book About Christopher Columbus by Ruth Belov Gross

The Boy Who Sailed with Columbus by Michael Foreman

Christopher Columbus by Ann McGovern

Christopher Columbus by Lisl Weil

Christopher Columbus: A Great Explorer by Carol Greene

Christopher Columbus: Great Explorer by David Adler

Columbus by Ingri and Edgar d'Aulaire

Columbus, Finder of the New World by Ronald Symer

The Columbus Story by Alice Dagliesh

The Discovery of the Americas by Betsy and Guilio Maestro

Encounter by Jane Yolen

The First Voyage of Christopher Columbus 1492 by Barry Smith

Follow the Dream: The Story of Christopher Columbus by Peter Sis

In 1492 by Jean Marzollo

The Great Adventure of Christopher Columbus by Jean Fritz

Meet Christopher Columbus by James T. deKay

My First Columbus Day Book by Dee Lillegard

Over the Rolling Sea by Alan Mills

A Picture Book of Christopher Columbus by David A. Adler

The Story of Christopher Columbus, Admiral of the Ocean Sea by Mary Pope Osborne

The Voyage of Columbus by Rupert Matthews

The Voyages of Christopher Columbus by Armstrong Sperry

Westward with Columbus by John Dyson

Where Do You Think You're Going, Christopher Columbus? by Jean Fritz

Language Experience

• How many words can your students make out of the letters in *Christopher Columbus*?

Writing Experience

• Discuss the types of provisions Columbus and his shipmates might have needed to take with them on their ships (charts, maps, compass, food). Then let students write about what they would need to take on such a journey today. See reproducible on page 70.

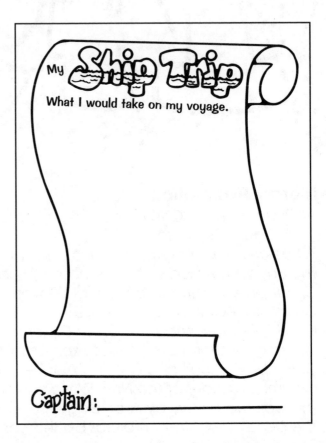

My **Ship Trip**

What I would take on my voyage.

Captain: _____

• Columbus kept a journal of each day's voyage. Challenge students to write an entry from Columbus' journal.

TLC10454 Copyright © Teaching & Learning Company, Carthage, IL 62321-0010

Math Experience

• Measure out the length of the *Santa Maria* (about 78 feet) with rope or yarn. Let students get inside it to get a perspective of the size of the ship.

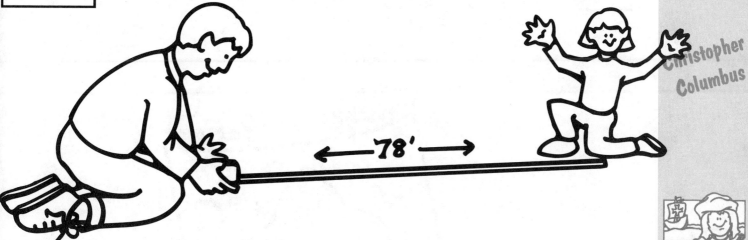

Science/Health Experience

• Experiment with various small items to see which will sink and which will float.

• Discuss the perception of the Earth's shape at the time of Columbus. Divide the class and host a debate. Let half the class try to convince the others that the Earth is flat as many believed in Columbus' time. The other half takes a stance that the Earth is round. Let students defend their positions.

Social Studies Experience

- Study the time period of Christopher Columbus, the events leading up to his voyage. Students may create a time line with the most significant events.

- Columbus had to understand the maps of his day. Review mapping skills with your class.

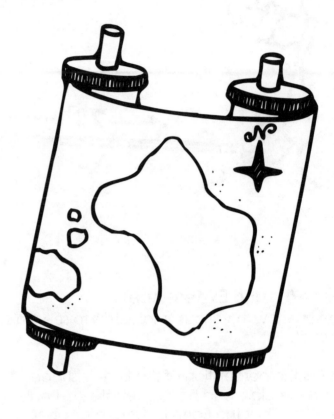

Music/Dramatic Experience

- Have students act out the events leading up to Columbus' voyage (such as requesting money and ships from the queen), the voyage itself and landing in the New World.

- Sing "In Fourteen Hundred Ninety-Two" by Stephen Fay.

TLC10454 Copyright © Teaching & Learning Company, Carthage, IL 62321-0010

Physical/Sensory Experience

• Columbus was anxious to obtain spices from the West Indies. Have a spice-smelling contest! Poke holes in the lids of plastic margarine tubs. Write labels for the spices. Dip a cotton ball into each spice and put it in a plastic tub. Let students sniff the mystery tubs and try to match the smells with the correct spice labels.

• Play *Hotter . . . Colder* with your students. Have one student be "Columbus" and stand outside the classroom while the rest of the students decide where the "West Indies" will be in your room. "Columbus" comes back in and students coach him as he moves around the room, saying "hotter" when he gets close and "colder" when he goes farther from their chosen spot.

Arts/Crafts Experience

• Let students make "telescopes" to search for the New World. In the end of a paper towel tube, punch holes with a hole punch. Tie yarn through to allow the telescope to be hung around the neck. Let students paint and decorate their telescopes or use the pattern on page 71.

Jr. Discoverer Telescope

Arts/Crafts Experience continued

- Provide large cardboard boxes such as refrigerator boxes from an appliance store. Let children paint and decorate the boxes to turn them into the *Nina, Pinta* and *Santa Maria.*

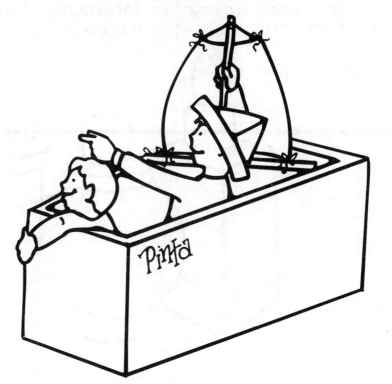

- Involve fast finishers in painting a mural of Columbus' voyage.

- Students will enjoy making Ships in a Bottle. Cut off the bottom fourth of a two-liter plastic bottle. Cut strips of blue plastic wrap and crinkle them to make waves on the horizontal bottom of a two-liter bottle lined with glue. Students can make the three ships to "drift" on the waves.

- Have students draw an ocean scene, and cut a slit in the middle of the ocean. Then they draw one of Columbus' ships, cut it out, glue it to a craft stick, and insert it into the slit. They can move the ship along the ocean.

- Let students paint blue tempera paint across a plain white sheet of construction paper. After it is dry, they can tear across the paper (lengthwise) in wave-like strips. They place these "waves" on the bottom half of another sheet of white construction paper for an ocean scene. Then they can draw a ship which can be cut out and slipped between the "waves" with a light blue sky overhead.

TLC10454 Copyright © Teaching & Learning Company, Carthage, IL 62321-0010

Arts/Crafts Experience continued

• A Columbus ship can easily be made from a walnut half. Have students place a small piece of clay in the bottom of the nut, then insert a paper sail on a toothpick into the clay.

• You may prefer to have students put clay in the bottom of a milk carton, then fasten a sail into the clay on a straw instead of a toothpick. Cut out a boat shape and trace another to match. Staple the sides of the boat together and insert the milk carton with the sails inside it. Cut the outline of waves in much the same way, stapling the bottom and sides. Put the entire boat inside the waves for a three-dimensional art project.

Extension Activities

• Serve treats of Italian sausage (Columbus was from Italy), Spanish peanuts (he sailed from Spain) and all-American apple pie (Columbus sailed to America). Let students eat their snacks on a sheet or blanket shaped like the *Nina, Pinta* or *Santa Maria*.

• Make popcorn balls to resemble the Earth, adding blue food coloring for water and green and brown m & m's™ for land.

"The Earth Is Round" Popcorn Balls

1/4 c. margarine

1 pkg. mini marshmallows

7-8 c. popcorn

Melt and mix margarine and marshmallows together. Add popcorn to mixture and stir.

Extension Activities continued

- Cut pieces of brown bread diagonally and place pretzel sticks in the cut side of the piece of bread. Position "sails" of flattened large marshmallows or white rectangular slices of white bread on the pretzel sticks.

- Display travel brochures and pamphlets (for samples) around a globe for an activity center. Let students "discover" new countries. Challenge each one to give his country a name, design a map of it and make travel brochures so others will want to set sail for it!

- Try yummy Columbus Day Banana Boats! Create banana splits with three scoops (one for each ship). On top of each scoop, add thin straws with alternating marshmallow and cherry "sails"!

Values Education Experience

- Check out the animated Christopher Columbus video from "Hero Classics" for your students to enjoy. (approximately 30 minutes)

TLC10454 Copyright © Teaching & Learning Company, Carthage, IL 62321-0010

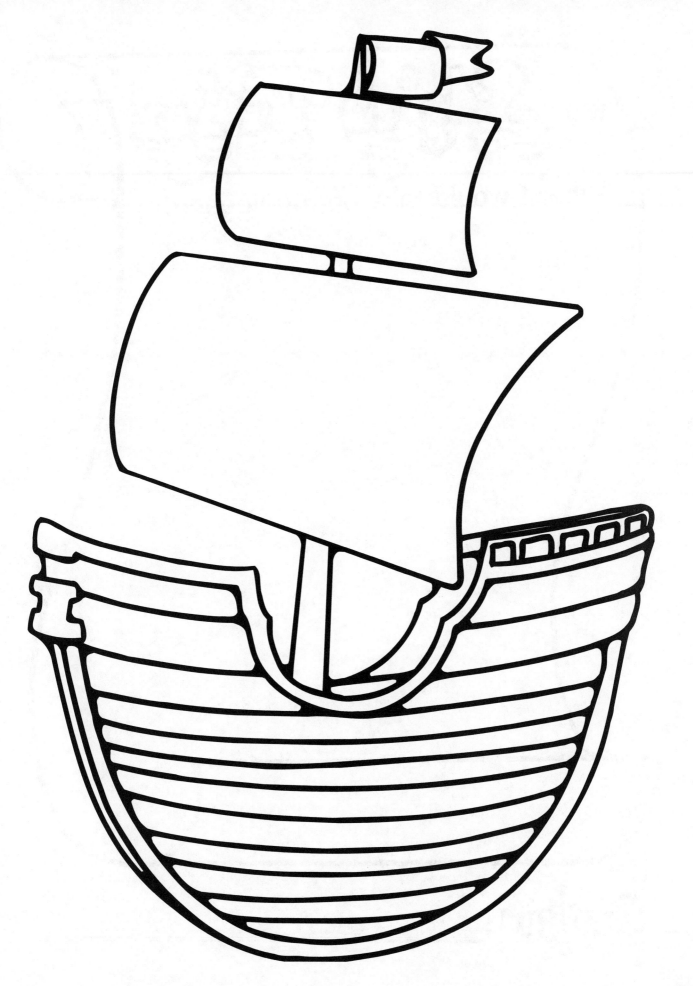

My **Ship Trip**

What I would take on my voyage.

Captain: _____

TLC10454 Copyright © Teaching & Learning Company, Carthage, IL 62321-0010

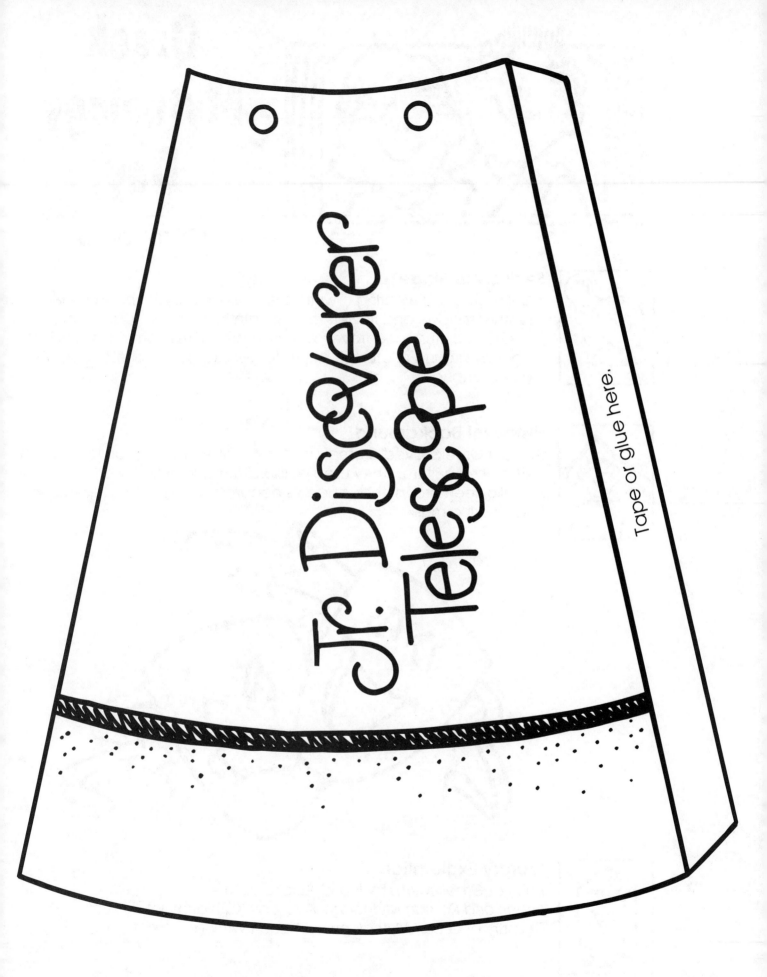

Jr. Discoverer Telescope

Tape or glue here.

TLC10454 Copyright © Teaching & Learning Company, Carthage, IL 62321-0010

Greek Mythology Day

October 13

Setting the Stage

• Greet students wearing a white sheet draped over one shoulder, leather sandals and flowers or a wreath in your hair. Display pictures of Greek culture and travel posters or brochures from a local travel agency around related literature to get students excited about the day's emphasis.

Historical Background

Ancient Greeks loved drama and the theatre. This was an important part of their culture. They used elaborate masks in their performances. As Halloween draws near, students become interested in dressing up and wearing masks.

Literary Exploration

Book of Greek Myths by Ingrid Aulaire
Greek and Roman Mythology A to Z by Kathleen Daly
Treasury of Greek Mythology by Alisoun Witting

TLC10454 Copyright © Teaching & Learning Company, Carthage, IL 62321-0010

Language Experience

• Aesop was a Greek slave credited with writing short tales known as "Aesop's Fables." Review the literary genre of fables and read some of Aesop's fables from your local library.

Writing Experience

• Let students write Greek adventure stories using characters from Greek mythology. They can write on a long piece of paper towel or on the patterns on page 77. Glue a thin dowel or craft stick on each end and roll it up for a Greek scroll.

Social Studies Experience

• Study Greek history and its culture. Locate Greece on a map. Create a time line with significant events in Greek history.

• Invite interested students to research famous Greeks throughout history: Socrates, Euripides, Homer, Sophocles, Plato and Alexander the Great.

Music/Dramatic Experience

• If your class makes Greek lyres (see Arts/Crafts Experience on page 75) today, allow some time for students to play their homemade instruments.

• Let students present Greek theatre! Review some of Aesop's fables or Greek mythology. Groups of students may act out stories for the rest of the class.

Greek
Mythology

Greek
Mythology

Greek
Mythology

Physical/Sensory Experience

- After studying Greek architecture, go on a neighborhood walk to look for homes or buildings that have architecture influenced by Greek style (such as columns or sculptured panels).

- Host a mini marathon in honor of the Greek race from Marathon to Athens in 1896. Adapt the length of the marathon to your students' ages and capacity. (It could be a lap around the playing field or a couple of miles.)

TLC10454 Copyright © Teaching & Learning Company, Carthage, IL 62321-0010

Arts/Crafts Experience

• Greek lyres were instruments similar to the harp used today. Tortoise shells were used to make the original Greek lyres. Students can make a homemade lyre with a metal coat hanger. Shape the coat hanger into a circle. Turn it upside down (so it resembles a balloon with a string hanging down). Shape the top two corners into "ears" so it looks like an animal head. Turn up the hook on the bottom into the center. Cut seven thin rubber bands. Tie each one between the stretched-out hook and the two "ears" on the top. These bands will produce the sound of the instrument. Give each student a paper plate to paint like a tortoise shell. It can be taped to the front of the instrument to cover the bent hook.

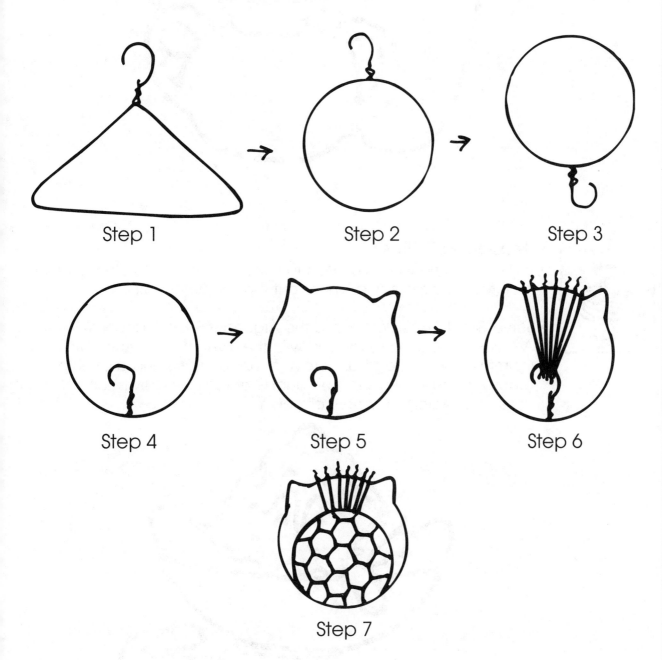

Step 1 → Step 2 → Step 3

Step 4 → Step 5 → Step 6

Step 7

Arts/Crafts Experience continued

• Since clay was abundant in Greece, potters produced all types of vessels in the form of vases, pitchers, jugs and jars. Let students try their hand at making a simple cup or pot.

Extension Activities

• Invite someone who has been to Greece to come to class and share pictures or artifacts and talk about this unique country.

• Serve Greek Splits: Jason and the Argonaut Ships (bananas) with Ambrosia (ice cream) topped with the River of Stix (syrup), Medusa (gummy worms), Pegasus' Grain (chopped nuts) and a Cyclops (cherry) on top. Serve in individual Grecian urns (bowls) and a cup of Poseidon (water) to wash it all down!

TLC10454 Copyright © Teaching & Learning Company, Carthage, IL 62321-0010

Glue craft stick here.

By: _____

Glue craft stick here.

Glue craft stick here.

By: _____

Glue craft stick here.

TLC10454 Copyright © Teaching & Learning Company, Carthage, IL 62321-0010

Something to "Crow" About Day

October 14

Setting the Stage

- Create a scarecrow from a pair of overalls or jeans and a plaid shirt. Stuff the clothes with pillows and old rags, sticking straw pieces around legs, neck and sleeves. The head can be a pumpkin or pillowcase decorated with permanent markers. A straw hat can add the final touch.

- Construct a semantic web with facts your students know (or would like to know) about crows and scarecrows to help you plan your day.

TLC10454 Copyright © Teaching & Learning Company, Carthage, IL 62321-0010

Literary Exploration

Don't Be Scared, Scarecrow by Pirkko Vainio
Emily and the Crows by Elaine Greenstein
Go Away Crows by Margo Mason
Johnny Crow's Garden (series) by L. Leslie Brooke
The Old Witch and the Crows by Ida deLage
The Scarebird by Sid Fleischman
Scarecrow Clock by George Mendoza
Six Crows by Leo Lionni
Tattercoats by Bernadette Watts
Two Crows Counting by Doris Orgel

Language Experience

• Let students brainstorm other words that have a long "o" sound, as in *crow*.

Math Experience

• Review geometric shapes with younger students. Let them make a scarecrow out of construction paper shapes (circle head, square body, rectangle legs and arms, and smaller circles for hands and feet). The facial details can also be created out of geometric shapes (eyes and rosy cheeks out of small circles, and a triangle nose). Add a triangle hat on top of the scarecrow head. After they cut and glue the pieces together, students can add yellow construction paper "straw" pieces (or raffia) coming out of the neck, arms and feet.

Music/Dramatic Experience

• If your class makes crow sock puppets (page 81), let them use their puppets to act out the children's fable, "The Crow and the Pitcher."

Physical/Sensory Experience

• Play a game of Crows and Cranes. Divide students into two groups (Crows and Cranes). Designate a "goal" for each. The two groups face one another, about five feet apart, as one group leader calls out the name of someone in the other group. That leader's group chases the person named as he tries to make it to his goal without being caught. If caught, he must go to the opposite team. Then the leader of the other team names someone. The team with the most members at the end of the game wins.

TLC10454 Copyright © Teaching & Learning Company, Carthage, IL 62321-0010

Arts/Crafts Experience

• Students can make black crow puppets! Provide (or ask each student to bring) a dark sock. With adult help, students use a hot glue gun to glue buttons for eyes and yellow or gold felt for beaks on the socks. Then students can manipulate the hand puppets to act out a skit or story.

Extension Activities

• Serve Scarecrow Shakes!

Scarecrow Shake

2¹/₂ c milk

3 ripe bananas

4 scoops of chocolate ice cream

1 c crushed ice

Mix the above ingredients
in a blender and serve
as soon as possible.

Follow-Up/Homework Idea

• Encourage students to look for scarecrows (scarecrow decorations) on the way home from school.

Machines and Things Day

October 15

Setting the Stage

- Display pictures of all kinds of machines around related literature to help engage the interest of students.

- Construct a semantic web with facts your students know (or would like to know) about machines to help plan the day.

Historical Background

A dirigible (somewhat like a hot-air balloon) made its first commercial flight from Germany to America on this date in 1928.

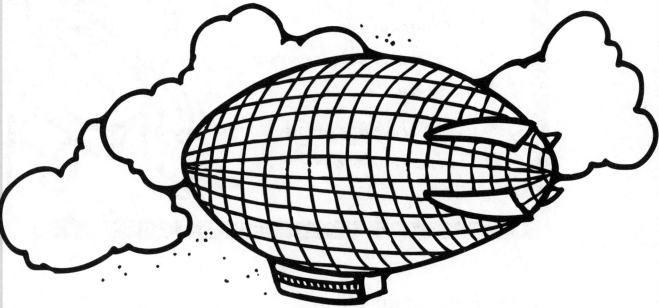

TLC10454 Copyright © Teaching & Learning Company, Carthage, IL 62321-0010

Literary Exploration

Alistairs' Time Machine by Marilyn Sadler
Bathtubs, Slides, Roller Coaster Rails by Christopher Lampton
Big Wheels by Anne Rockwell
Cars and How They Go by Joanna Cole
The Extraordinary Invention by Bernice Myers
Heavy Equipment by Jan Adkins
Machines by Harlow and Anne Rockwell
Machines at Work by Byron Barton
Marbles, Roller Skates, Doorknobs by Christopher Lampton
Mike Mulligan and the Steam Shovel by Virginia Burton
Sailboats, Flagpoles, Cranes: Using Pulleys by Christopher Lampton
Science Fun with Toy Cars and Trucks by Rose Wyler
Seesaws, Nutcrackers, Brooms: Simple Machines by Christopher Lampton
Simple Facts of Simple Machines by Elizabeth James
Simple Machines by Anne Horvatic
Things That Go by Random House
Tom and Pippo and the Washing Machine by Helen Oxenbury
The True Book of Transportation by Elsa Posell
The Way Things Work by David MacCaulay
Wheels: A Book to Begin On by Eleanor Clymer
Wheels Across America by Terry Shannon
The Wheels on the Bus by Maryann Kovalski

Language Experience

• Let students brainstorm as many forms of transportation as they can, then list them in alphabetical order.

Writing Experience

- Ask students to imagine that they are in a time machine that can take them back (or forward) in time. Have them write about which way they would go and to tell about their adventures. See reproducible on page 87.

Science/Health Experience

- Review safety precautions when working with (or around) any type of machinery.

- Today is a perfect day to begin a science unit on simple machines (pulley, lever, wedge, wheel and axle, inclined plane) discussing how they make our work easier.

TLC10454 Copyright © Teaching & Learning Company, Carthage, IL 62321-0010

Machines
and
Things

Machines
and
Things

Machines
and
Things

Social Studies Experience

• Explore the history of transportation and depict important inventions involving modes of transportation on a time line.

Music/Dramatic Experience

• Sing the children's favorite, "The Wheels on the Bus."

• Let younger children pretend to be various forms of transportation (from a tugboat to a spaceship).

Physical/Sensory Experience

• Provide several examples of simple machines at a science center (screwdriver, can opener, egg beater) so students can manipulate each one to see for themselves how it works.

Extension Activities

• Invite a machinist to come and talk about his or her work.

• Let students create Edible Simple Machines out of finger foods (cracker wedges, pretzel and marshmallow hammers, cheese chunk inclined planes, chocolate sandwich cookie wheels).

Follow-Up/Homework Idea

• Challenge students to see how many simple machines they can find in their homes and garages.

TLC10454 Copyright © Teaching & Learning Company, Carthage, IL 62321-0010

Time Machine Adventures

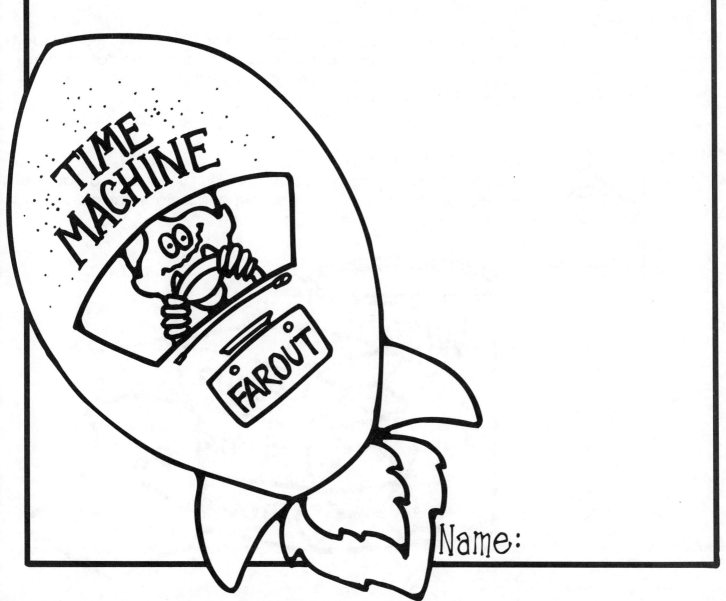

TIME MACHINE

FAROUT

Name:

LC10454 Copyright © Teaching & Learning Company, Carthage, IL 62321-0010

World Food Day

October 16

Setting the Stage

- Draw a wide-open mouth and display it on the board with the caption: "Everybody Open Wide for Good Food!" Invite students to draw pictures of nutritious foods to put inside the mouth. For a variation of this, let students place pictures of food in individual train cars with a train labeled, *Hop Aboard the Food Train!* This can be made into a bulletin board display.

- Divide a sheet of poster board in half. Label one half, *Healthy Foods* and the other, *Not-So-Healthy Foods*. Throughout the day, students can cut out magazine pictures of food and place them in the appropriate column.

Historical Background

The United Nations designated October 16th as World Food Day. It is a day set aside to recognize world hunger and increase awareness for solving this problem.

TLC10454 Copyright © Teaching & Learning Company, Carthage, IL 62321-0010

Literary Exploration

Alexander's Midnight Snack by Catherine Stock
The Berenstain Bears and Too Much Junk Food by Stan Berenstain
Cloudy with a Chance of Meatballs by Ron and Judi Barrett
Good for Me!: All About Food in 32 Bites by Marilyn Burns
Gregory, the Terrible Eater by Mitchell Sharmat
Mealtime by Maureen Roffey
My Very First Book of Food by Eric Carle
Nutrition (A New True Book) by Leslie Jean LeMaster
Nutrition: What's in the Food We Eat by Dorothy Hinshaw Patent
The Very Hungry Caterpillar by Eric Carle
What Happens to a Hamburger? by Paul Showers
Yummers! by James Marshall
Yummers Two: The Second Course by James Marshall

Writing Experience

• Let students write about what they like and don't like to eat and why. Students usually form strong opinions about food at an early age. See reproducible on page 92.

Name: _____

My favorite things to eat are...

• Encourage students to study a food pyramid, then write a balanced menu for a given meal.

• Let students write silly stories about how to use leftover food. (Example: Brussels sprout as a paperweight)

Math Experience

- Let students survey other students about their favorite foods, then add the information to a class bar graph.

Science/Health Experience

- Today is a good day to begin a health unit on nutrition.

- Students will be interested in what happens to food in the digestion process. Read Paul Showers' book, *What Happens to a Hamburger?* Let them simulate the digestive process with this fun activity. Give each student a small plastic bag with a corner cut off. Spoon a small serving of pudding into each bag. Have them attempt to push the pudding through the hole onto a piece of wax paper, simulating the involuntary movement of the esophagus pushing food through to the stomach. Students can finger paint with the resulting "digested"

Social Studies Experience

- Discuss the world hunger problem. Let students share their ideas about how this global situation can be solved.

Music/Dramatic Experience

- Let students go "shopping" for good food. Provide food from all food groups. Label grocery bags with food group labels, such as *Breads and Cereals*. Students shop for items to go in the appropriately labeled bags. For fun, add a trashcan for sugary or salty snacks.

TLC10454 Copyright © Teaching & Learning Company, Carthage, IL 62321-001

Physical/Sensory Experience

- Play Run for Your Supper. Students sit in a circle as a person who is designated as "It" walks around them. When "It" stops between two students and says, "Run for your supper," the two students run in opposite directions around the outside of the circle, trying to get to the place left by the other runner. "It" sits down in one of the empty places. The person left without a place to sit becomes the new "It."

Arts/Crafts Experience

- Let students design new packages or containers for healthful snacks they dream up.

- Have students cut pictures of food from magazines and make a food collage.

- Provide paper plates or a pattern for a lunch food tray. Let students plan their dream lunch, then cut out pictures of foods from the various food groups to place on the plate or tray to create a well-balanced, nutritious meal. The pattern on page 92 may also be used for this activity.

Extension Activities

- Set up a nutritious snack tasting table. Students can bring in their favorite nutritious finger foods to share. (Be mindful of any food allergies or restrictions your students may have.)

- Host a canned food drive, collecting food for the needy. Donate it to a local homeless shelter or food pantry.

Follow-Up/Homework Idea

- Challenge students to create a nutritious after-school snack when they get home.

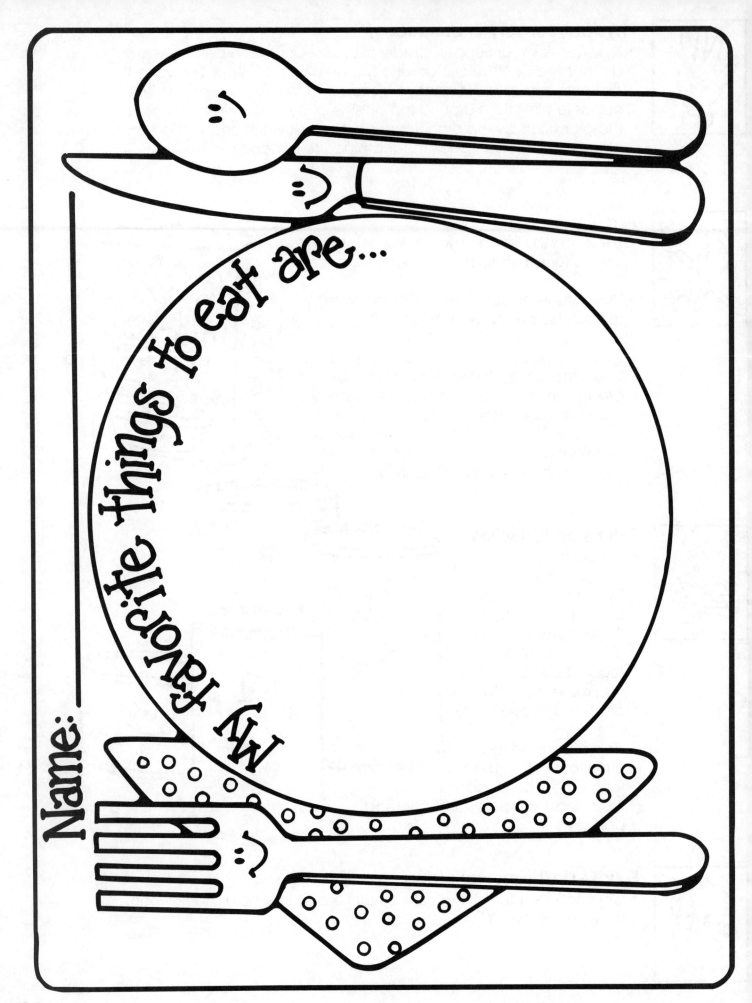

Name:

My favorite things to eat are...

TLC10454 Copyright © Teaching & Learning Company, Carthage, IL 62321-001

Mummies and Pyramids Day

October 17

Setting the Stage

- Your students will get "all wrapped up" in today's activities! Display pictures of Egyptian pyramids, mummies and travel posters or brochures around related literature to engage their interest.

- Construct a semantic web with words your students think of when you say, "mummy" or "pyramid."

Historical Background

The ancient Egyptians are known for their efforts to preserve the dead through the mummies and artifacts which have been discovered in pyramids and other burial sites.

LC10454 Copyright © Teaching & Learning Company, Carthage, IL 62321-0010

Literary Exploration

Egyptian Pyramids by Anne Steel
Egyptian Tombs by Jeanne Bendick
The Giant Book of the Mummy by Rosalie David
Hey Willy, See the Pyramid by Maira Kalman
Into the Mummy's Tomb: The Real-Life Discovery of Tutankhamun's Treasures by Nicholas Reeves
I Wonder Why Pyramids Were Built? by Phillip Steel
Learning About Mummies by Laura Alden
The Man-Made Wonders of the World by Dorothy Turner
M & M and the Mummy Mess by Pat Ross
Mummies Made in Egypt by Aliki
Mummies, Tombs and Treasure by Lila Perl
Pyramid by David MacCaulay
Pyramids by Claude Delafosse
Pyramids by Anne Millard
Secrets of the Mummies by Joyce Milton
Tut's Mummy, Lost and Found by Judy Donelly
Where's Julius? by John Burningham

Language Experience

• Teach students how to build words with word pyramids! Have them write their spelling words on a sheet of paper leaving room above each word. Show them how to begin at the bottom and work up, deleting a letter at the end of each line until they have a pyramid shape.

```
      p
     py
    pyr
   pyra
  pyram
 pyrami
pyramid
```

Writing Experience

• Bring in a small rug. Have students imagine that it is a "magic carpet" and can take them anywhere in the world. Invite them to write about where they would like to go and describe their adventures on their magic carpet. See reproducible on page 97.

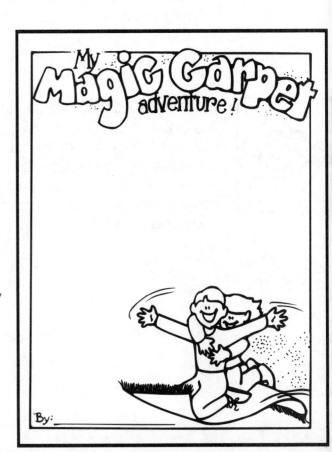

My **Magic Carpet** adventure!

By:_____

94

Science/Health Experience

• Today is a great day to review a health unit on the food "pyramid."

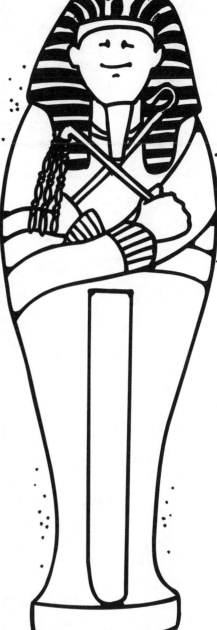

Social Studies Experience

• Study the history and culture of Ancient Egypt.

• Let interested students research some of the pharaohs of Egypt (such as nine-year-old King Tut who only lived to age 19). Students can share their information with the rest of the class.

Physical/Sensory Experience

• Play the Mummy Relay! Divide the class into relay teams. Give each team a roll of white toilet paper. At the signal, students race to completely wrap one of their members as a "mummy" before time is up.

• Group students in teams of three and let them try to make human pyramids (two students on hands and knees on the bottom, one on hands and knees on top of the two). This activity needs careful adult monitoring and gym mats to avoid mishaps.

LC10454 Copyright © Teaching & Learning Company, Carthage, IL 62321-0010

Mummies
and
Pyramids

Mummies
and
Pyramids

Mummies
and
Pyramids

Arts/Crafts Experience

• Borrow a book about hieroglyphics from a local library (such as Catherine Roehrig's *Fun with Hieroglyphics*). Then let students try their hand at this unique picture writing.

• Let students wrap a miniature mummy. Hand out wooden clothespins (the type with a rounded head) and long strips of white cloth. They can wrap the cloth around the clothespin and draw facial details on the head.

Extension Activities

• Serve a Middle Eastern treat such as honey on pita bread or figs. If you can't find figs, serve Fig Newtons™. (Be mindful of any food allergies or restrictions your students may have.)

• Invite a local archaeologist to come and talk about his or her work.

Values Education Experience

• Talk about the jewelry and treasures that have been discovered in Egyptian tombs. Your local library may have a photo resource on King Tut's treasures or museum collections (such as New York's Metropolitan Museum of Art or the Cairo Museum).

Follow-Up/Homework Idea

• Invite students to get "all wrapped up" in a new book tonight.

TLC10454 Copyright © Teaching & Learning Company, Carthage, IL 62321-001

My Magic Carpet adventure!

By: _____

TLC10454 Copyright © Teaching & Learning Company, Carthage, IL 62321-0010

"Hoot" & Nanny Day

October 18

Setting the Stage

• Display student work around an image of an owl with a caption that reads, "Guess WHOOO's Working Hard?"

• Construct a semantic web with facts your students already know (or would like to know) about owls to help you structure your day's activities.

Literary Exploration

About Owls by May Garelick
Goodnight, Owl! by Pat Hutchins
The Great Horned Owl by Lynn Stone
The Great White Owl of Sissinghurst by Dawn Langley Simmons
Happy Birthday Owl by Paul Dowling
Kiou, the Owl by Vassilissa
Mouse and Owl by Joan Hoffman
Mrs. Owl and Mr. Pig by Jan Wahl
Owl and the Woodpecker by Brian Wildsmith
An Owl and Three Pussycats by Alice Provensen
Owl at Home by Arnold Lobel
Owl Babies by Martin Waddell
The Owl Book by Laura Storms
Owliver by Robert Krauss
Owl Lake by Tejima Keizburo
Owl Moon by Jane Yolen
Owls in the Family by Farley Mowatt
Owls in the Garden by Berniece Freschet
The Owl Who Became the Moon by Jonathan London
Snappity Snap by Stephen Wyllie
Tiger with Wings by Barbara Juster Esbensen
Your Owl Friend by Crescent Dragonwagon

TLC10454 Copyright © Teaching & Learning Company, Carthage, IL 62321-0010

Language Experience

• Have students brainstorm other words that have the "ow" sound as in the word *owl*.

Writing Experience

• Choose a topic and let students write some "Wise Tips" (for example: Energy Conservation, Behavior in the Lunchroom, Halloween Safety, etc.). See reproducible on page 101.

Wise tips for

Name: _____

Science/Health Experience

• Learn about owls and their habitat.

• Discuss sleeping preferences and what it means to be a "night owl."

• Talk about Woodsy the Owl's motto, "Give a Hoot, Don't Pollute." Discuss solutions to environmental pollution. Students might want to raise awareness by making "Give a Hoot, Don't Pollute" posters and displaying them around the school.

"Hoot" & Nanny

"Hoot" & Nanny

"Hoot" & Nanny

Arts/Crafts Experience
• Students can make a three-dimensional stuffed owl by filling a paper lunch bag with newspaper (for the body) and tying the bottom with a piece of yarn (for the feet). They can add construction paper eyes, beak, wings, ears and tail.

Values Education Experience
• Discuss the meaning of the familiar saying: "Be as wise as an owl."

Follow-Up/Homework Idea
• Challenge students to be as wise as they are kind.

TLC10454 Copyright © Teaching & Learning Company, Carthage, IL 62321-0010

Wise tips for

Name: _____

TLC10454 Copyright © Teaching & Learning Company, Carthage, IL 62321-0010

Red Ribbon Day

October 19

Setting the Stage

• Display student self-portraits with speech balloons coming from their mouths as if they are speaking. In the speech balloons, students can write what they would say if someone offered them drugs, tobacco or alcohol.

• Construct a semantic web with words your students think of when you say the word *drug*.

Historical Background

Traditionally, the last part of October, between the 19th and 26th, is a national kickoff for Red Ribbon Week in schools throughout the nation. The Red Ribbon Week campaign began as a result of the unfortunate death of Federal Agent Enrique Camarena in 1985. The symbol of a red ribbon was suggested to schools as a way to encourage drug prevention among youth. Later, a purple ribbon was added to the campaign to represent violence prevention in Red Ribbon Week activities.

TLC10454 Copyright © Teaching & Learning Company, Carthage, IL 62321-0010

Literary Exploration

The Emperor's New Clothes by Hans Christian Andersen
How to Eat Fried Worms by Thomas Rockwell
Just Say No: A Book About Saying "No" to Drugs by Barbara Shook Hazen
Say No and Know Why: Kid's Learn About Drugs by Wendy Way
What Are Drugs? by Gretchen Super
You Can Say "No" to Drugs by Gretchen Super

Writing Experience

• Have students write what they would say if someone offered them drugs or alcohol. See reproducible on page 105.

What would I say?

Name: _____

Science/Health Experience

• Begin a health unit on making responsible choices about drugs, alcohol and tobacco.

TLC10454 Copyright © Teaching & Learning Company, Carthage, IL 62321-0010

Red Ribbon

Red Ribbon

Red Ribbon

Social Studies Experience

- After reading, Hans Christian Andersen's *The Emperor's New Clothes*, or Thomas Rockwell's *How to Eat Fried Worms*, discuss peer pressure.

Red
Ribbon

Music/Dramatic Experience

- Sing "The Choice for Me-Drug Free!" (lyrics by Jay Ball, music by Elaine Clarke).

- Borrow Janeen Brady's sound recording of *Safety Kid's* "Play It Smart, Stay Safe from Drugs" from a local library.

- Get students involved in role-playing situations where they are asked to experiment with drugs, alcohol or tobacco. They can show how they would say "no" in a variety of ways.

Physical/Sensory Experience

- Explain how much better it is to enjoy a natural "high" (from fun, active life-style, enjoying one's interests and hobbies) rather than a chemical "high." Enjoy some time outside with your students, letting them see your playful side.

Red
Ribbon

Arts/Crafts Experience

- Let students design posters urging other students to stay drug-free. These can be posted throughout the school.

Extension Activities

- If your class reads Thomas Rockwell's *How to Eat Fried Worms*, be sure to serve "gummy worms" for a fun treat!

Red
Ribbon

Follow-Up/Homework Idea

- Challenge students to be committed to a drug-free life-style!

TLC10454 Copyright © Teaching & Learning Company, Carthage, IL 62321-0010

What would I say?

Name: _____

TLC10454 Copyright © Teaching & Learning Company, Carthage, IL 62321-0010

Bela Lugosi's Birthday

October 20

Setting the Stage
• Display Halloween masks and related literature to gather interest in today's activities.

• Talk about theatrical makeup and masks.

Historical Background
Bela Lugosi was a well-known character actor famous for his many villainous roles including monsters, mad scientists and Dracula.

Literary Exploration
Horror Films by Rhoda Nottridge

TLC10454 Copyright © Teaching & Learning Company, Carthage, IL 62321-0010

Language Experience

• Challenge students to see how many new words they can make using the letters in the name *Bela Lugosi.*

Science/Health Experience

• This is a perfect day to review Halloween safety for trick-or-treating.

Social Studies Experience

• Review places around the world where masks are made and worn by various tribes (such as, Native American or African ceremonial masks).

Music/Dramatic Experience

• Let students debate the pros and cons of wearing a Halloween mask versus Halloween makeup.

Physical/Sensory Experience

• Play a variation of the traditional Pin the Tail on the Donkey with Pin the Mask on the Face. Any Halloween mask can be pinned to a simple drawing of a face. See patterns on pages 109 and 110.

Arts/Crafts Experience

• This would be a great day to make papier-mache or construction paper masks.

Extension Activities

• Invite a local makeup artist to visit and show the process involved in theatrical makeup. Perhaps the artist could put some makeup on interested students.

Values Education Experience

• Discuss the invisible masks people sometimes wear to protect themselves.

Follow-Up/Homework Idea

• Encourage students to work out last-minute details for their Halloween costumes.

TLC10454 Copyright © Teaching & Learning Company, Carthage, IL 62321-0010

TLC10454 Copyright © Teaching & Learning Company, Carthage, IL 62321-0010

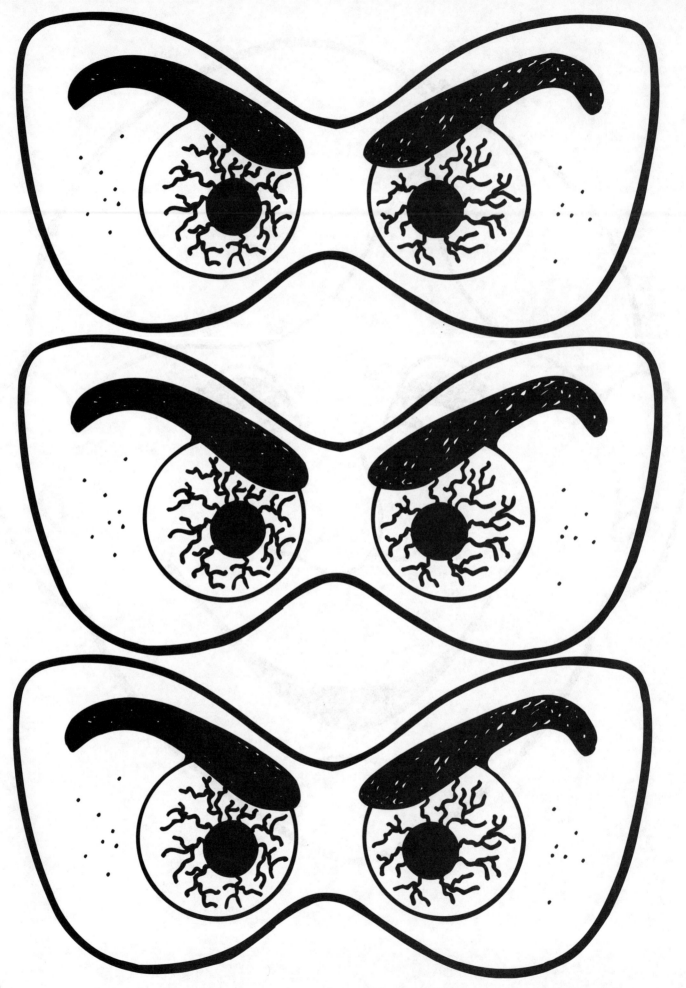

110

TLC10454 Copyright © Teaching & Learning Company, Carthage, IL 62321-0010

Ghostly Fun Day

October 21

Setting the Stage

• Display an image of a large ghost with student work around it and the caption: "WHOOOOOOOO Did This Great Work?" or, "It Just GHOST to Show You What a Smart Student YOOOOO ARE!"

• Draw ghost faces with black markers on white helium-filled balloons. Suspend the balloons from the ceiling.

Literary Exploration

Can't Scare Me! by Melissa Milich
Did You Say Ghosts? by Richard Michelson
Five Funny Frights by Judith Stamper
Georgie (series) by Robert Bright
Ghost-Eye Tree by Bill Martin Jr. and John Archambault
The Ghost Family Meets Its Match by Nicole Rubel
Ghost Games by Jana Hunter
Ghost in a Four-Room Apartment by Ellen Raskin
The Ghost's Dinner by Jacques Duquennoy
Ghost's Hour, Spook's Hour by Eve Bunting
Gus and the Baby Ghost (series) by Jane Thayer
Look Out for Ghosts! by Annette Tison
Slightly Spooky Stories by Michael Teitelbaum
Timothy and the Night Noises by Jeffrey Dinardo
Two Ghosts on a Bench by Marjorie Weinman Sharmat
What's a Ghost Going to Do? by Jane Thayer
Who's Afraid of Ghosts? by Bonnie Bader

Language Experience

• How many words can your students think of that rhyme with the word *ghost*?

Writing Experience

• Ask students to imagine what a ghost might say. Hand out large pieces of white tissue paper and long pieces of black string. Students arrange the string in the shape of a ghost on the tissue paper, then write a "ghostly" message in black marker in the center of the ghost. Put newspaper under the tissue so marker or glue does not bleed through. After students have written their messages, they can squeeze a thin line of glue on top of the string and it will dry to form a structured outline of a ghost. Students might need to shift the newspaper from time to time so the glue does not stick to the newspaper. They can cut out black construction paper eyes and mouth to glue on each ghost's face. When the glue is dry, have them cut the ghosts out, leaving a 1/2" border around the string. Tape black string to the top of the ghosts and hang them from the ceiling over each student's desk. Each student will have his own "haunted" desk!

TLC10454 Copyright © Teaching & Learning Company, Carthage, IL 62321-0010

Music/Dramatic Experience

• From a local library, borrow a sound recording of the soundtrack for the movie *Ghostbusters* to play for your students.

Physical/Sensory Experience

• Turn out the lights and tell tame ghost stories, nothing too scary. Include a few mild-mannered ghost tales from *Slightly Spooky Stories* by Michael Teitelbaum.

Arts/Crafts Experience

• Give each student a Tootsie Pop™ and a facial tissue to make a Lollipop Ghost. Students wrap the tissue over the lollipop, secure it with ribbon or yarn and draw on a ghost face.

• To make a Ghost Mobile, students can make four Lollipop Ghosts and string them from two criss-crossed craft sticks they have stapled together.

• Students will love making Cheesecloth Ghosts! Give each student a paper cup and a three-inch Styrofoam™ ball. Place the cup upside down and put the Styrofoam™ ball on top of it. Give each a piece of cheesecloth to drape over the Styrofoam™ ball and shape into a "ghost." Spray it with a thick coat of spray starch and let it dry. (Liquid starch can also be used, drenching the cheesecloth in a bowl of starch, then squeezing out the excess liquid.) Students can glue on black construction paper (or felt) facial details when the ghost is completely dry. The next day the cup and ball can be removed and the ghost will stand on its own or can be suspended from the ceiling.

Extension Activities

• Make a "ghostly" delicious pie! Mix chocolate pudding and pour it into a graham cracker crust. After the pudding is firmly set, pipe whipped cream topping from a cake decorator bag in the shape of a ghost on top of the pudding. Add chocolate chips for eyes and serve!

TLC10454 Copyright © Teaching & Learning Company, Carthage, IL 62321-0010

Monster Mania Day

October 22

Setting the Stage
- Display student work around the image of a silly-looking monster with the caption: "Creature Features."

- Construct a semantic web with words your students think of when you say the word *monster*.

Literary Exploration
Clyde Monster by Robert L. Crowe
The Frankenbagel Monster by Daniel Manus Pinkwater
Go Away, Big Green Monster! by Ed Emberley
A Halloween Mask for Monster by Virginia Mueller
Harry and the Terrible Whatzit by Dick Gackenbach
How Do You Hide a Monster? by Virginia Caroline Kahl
I Am a Monster by Joseph Mathieu
I'm Coming to Get You by Tony Ross
Ira Sleeps Over by Bernard Waber
I Wouldn't Be Scared by John Sabraw
Looking After Your First Monster by Frank Rodgers
*Making Friends with Frankenstein: A Book of Monstrous Poems and
    Pictures* by Colin McNaughton
The Marigold Monster by M.C. Delaney, et al
Monster (series) by Virginia Mueller
Monster Mama by Liz Rosenberg
The Monster Under My Bed by Suzanne Gruber
*My Mama Says There Aren't Any Zombies, Ghosts, Vampires, Creatures,
    Demons, Monsters, Fiends, Goblins or Things* by Judith Viorst
One Hungry Monster by Susan Heyboer
O'Keefe Shriek by William Steig
Skateboard Monsters by Daniel Kirk
The Something by Natalie Babbitt
Ten Green Monsters by Gus Clarke
There's a Monster Under My Bed by James Howe
There's a Nightmare in My Closet by Mercer Mayer
Where the Wild Things Are by Maurice Sendak

Language Experience

- Draw a picture of a monster with a very large mouth on the board, or make a monster from poster board and attach it to a trashcan "mouth." Ask students to "feed" the monster with certain word sounds such as: blends and digraphs or compound words. Reinforce what you are currently studying with this fun idea.

Writing Experience

- Have students write, using descriptive words, what a zombie looks like. Ask each to give the zombie a name and tell where it lives, what it likes to eat and what it does for fun.

- After reading Robert L. Crowe's *Clyde Monster*, let students write about what they think monsters are afraid of. See reproducible on page 123.

What are MONSTERS afraid of?

Name:_____

TLC10454 Copyright © Teaching & Learning Company, Carthage, IL 62321-0010

Math Experience

• If your class participated in feeding the monster (page 116) certain sounds or words, next they can feed it math numbers (numbers that add up to 18, odd numbers or what you are currently teaching).

Music/Dramatic Experience

• Borrow the favorite sound recording from a local library of Boris Karloff singing "The Monster Mash." Flick the lights on and off as students dance to this fun song!

• After reading Maurice Sendak's *Where the Wild Things Are*, let students act out the parts. Extra students can be the "Wild Things." Let them practice "rolling their terrible eyes" and "gnashing their terrible teeth." Students can take turns being "King of All the Wild Things." "Wild Thing" puppets can be made by folding a paper plate in half, adding egg carton eyes and scraggly yarn hair and glueing a red tongue between the halves.

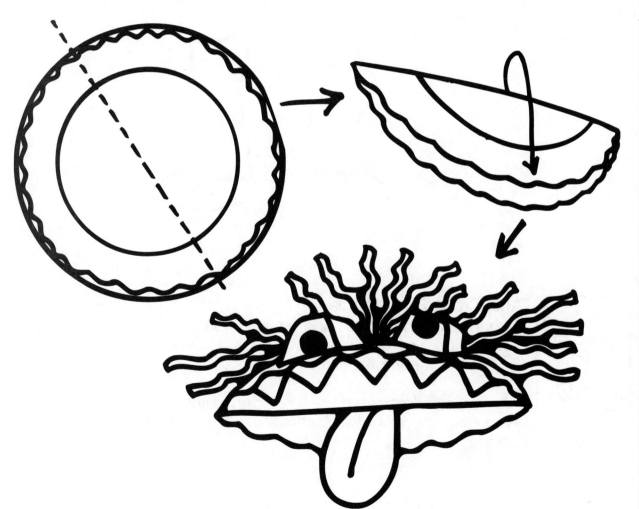

Physical/Sensory Experience

• Play Blob Tag! Choose one student to be the "Blob" who tries to tag others. Each time the "Blob" tags someone, that person joins hands with him or her. The Blob gradually gets bigger and bigger, but must keep tagging others (which is more difficult due to its size). The game ends when everyone is finally part of the "Blob."

• Pair up students. Partners turn back to back while one describes an imaginary monster. The other partner draws the monster as it is described. Then they trade roles and do it again.

Arts/Crafts Experience

• Hand out paper plates and art materials, such as: felt scraps, buttons, yarn, pipe cleaners and plastic bugs. Have students create original monster faces on the plates.

• For eerie-looking monsters, let students draw with colored chalk that has been dipped in white tempera paint on black construction paper.

TLC10454 Copyright © Teaching & Learning Company, Carthage, IL 62321-0010

Arts/Crafts Experience continued

- Have students fold art paper into three horizontal sections. They draw a monster head in the top section, a body in the middle and legs and feet in the bottom section. Then they cut apart the sections and trade them with other students. They can be rearranged into very unusual monsters. They make a great bulletin board display. See reproducible on page 124.

- Form student pairs and let each trace the other's body outline onto butcher paper. Then they can draw monster features on the body with white crayon. Wash over the crayon with watercolors. Let dry. Then have them cut out their monsters (including eye, nose and mouth openings) and tape them to their own bodies before going on a monster parade around the school.

Extension Activities

• How about making FrankenFEETers? Mix up a batch of rice cereal treats and let students form them into foot shapes. They can press gumdrop halves onto the feet for toenails. (Be mindful of any food allergies or restrictions your students my have.)

• Students will enjoy decorating sugar cookies, making them into monster faces. Prepare the refrigerator cookie dough as indicated on the package. Let students decorate the cooled cookies with icing, candies, nuts and raisins.

• Students can also decorate bread and peanut butter. Have them spread peanut butter on the bread, then add raisins, olives, fruit or raw vegetables for monster features. Serve with a Monster Milk Shake.

Monster Milk Shake

Blend the following in a blender:

1 c ice cream or sherbet

3 c orange juice

Any fresh or frozen fruit

120

Extension Activities continued

- Your students will love these Vampire Eyeballs! Place green grapes in an ice cube tray, then fill the tray with cranberry juice. Let the cubes freeze, then remove them by placing the bottom of the tray in a bowl of warm water. Students can place their Vampire Eyeballs in cups of grape juice for a very interesting effect! (Make sure to remove grapes from cups before students take a sip to avoid the choking hazard.)

- Serve Monster Mix! Have students draw monster heads, then staple them to zipped plastic bags. Add black beetles (raisins), vampire teeth (candy corn), shrunken skulls (mini marshmallows), slimy snake skins (gummy worms) and skeleton parts (pretzels) to the bag. See patterns on page 125.

Monster Mix!
- Black beetles
- Shrunken skulls
- Slimy snake skins
- Vampire teeth
- Skeleton parts
- Red goblin eyes

TLC10454 Copyright © Teaching & Learning Company, Carthage, IL 62321-0010

Extension Activities

• Let students make a batch of Gobbledy Gook! Provide baggies for them to place over their hands for sanitary purposes. Cut the tops off clean quart milk cartons to hold the mixture. Follow the recipe below.

Gobbledy Gook

2 c oatmeal, 1 c roasted peanuts*, 1 c candy corn, 1 c light corn syrup, 8 squares of semisweet chocolate

In a large bowl, combine oatmeal, peanuts and candy corn. Bring syrup to a boil and remove from heat. Stir in chocolate. Pour over oatmeal mixture and toss. Firmly pack the mixture into the milk carton. Cover and refrigerate for a couple of hours. Peel off carton and cut into slices and then squares. *Can be omitted if any of your students have food allergies.

Follow-Up/Homework Idea

• For a homework assignment, ask your students to count how many states start with the letter "M."

TLC10454 Copyright © Teaching & Learning Company, Carthage, IL 62321-001

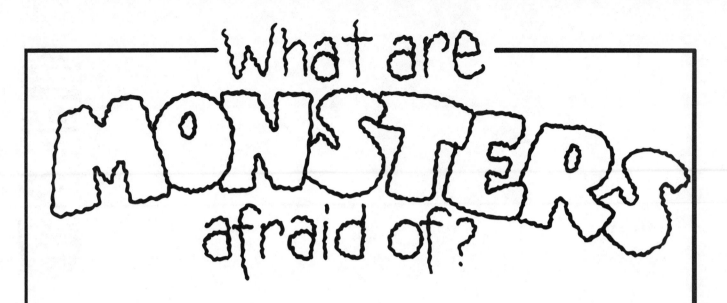

What are MONSTERS afraid of?

Name: _____

TLC10454 Copyright © Teaching & Learning Company, Carthage, IL 62321-0010

TLC10454 Copyright © Teaching & Learning Company, Carthage, IL 62321-001

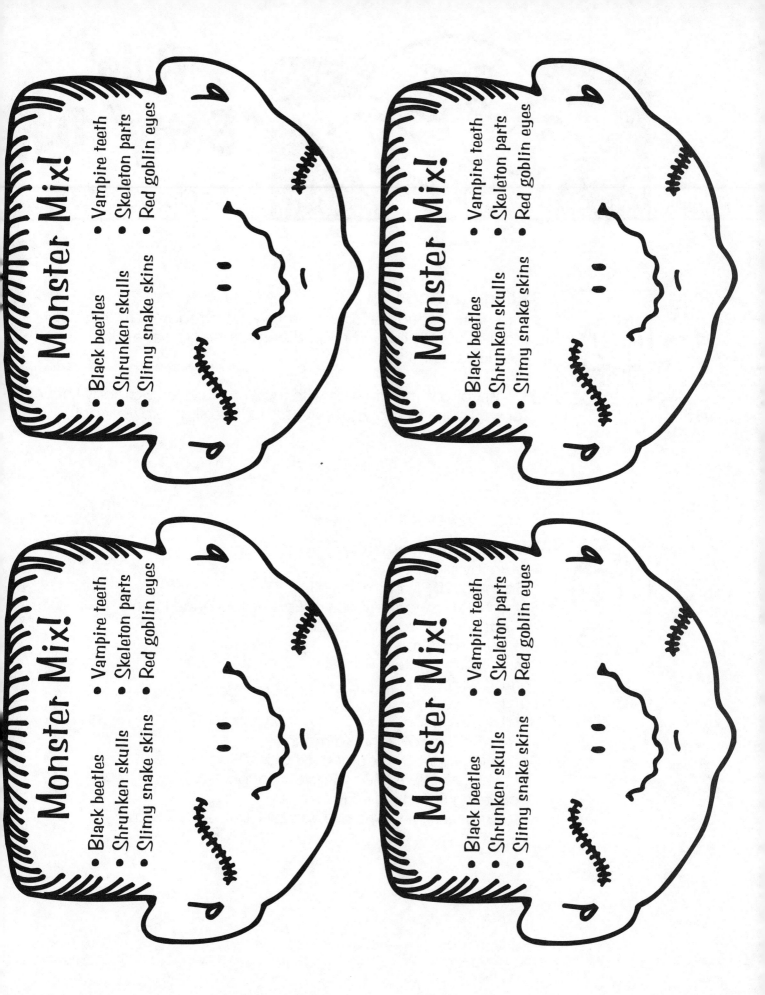

Monster Mix!
- Black beetles
- Vampire teeth
- Shrunken skulls
- Skeleton parts
- Slimy snake skins
- Red goblin eyes

Monster Mix!
- Black beetles
- Vampire teeth
- Shrunken skulls
- Skeleton parts
- Slimy snake skins
- Red goblin eyes

Monster Mix!
- Black beetles
- Vampire teeth
- Shrunken skulls
- Skeleton parts
- Slimy snake skins
- Red goblin eyes

Monster Mix!
- Black beetles
- Vampire teeth
- Shrunken skulls
- Skeleton parts
- Slimy snake skins
- Red goblin eyes

Goin' "Batty" Day

October 23

Setting the Stage

• Drive your students absolutely "batty" with today's emphasis! Display pictures of bats around related literature to gather excitement about the day's activities.

• Construct a semantic web with facts your students already know (or would like to know) about bats to help structure your day.

Literary Exploration

The Bat by Nina Leen
A Bat Is Born by Randall Jerrell
Batman: Exploring the World of Bats by Laurence Pringle
The Bat Poet by Randall Jerrell
Bats by Susan Gray
Bats by Alice Lightner Hopf
Bats by Sylvia Johnson
Bats by David Pye
Bats by Dee Stuart
Bats in the Dark by John Kafmann
Bats in the Night by George Laycock
Bats: Wings in the Night by Patricia Lauber
Discovering Bats by Jane Mulleneux
Eyewitness Juniors: Amazing Bats by Frank Greenaway

TLC10454 Copyright © Teaching & Learning Company, Carthage, IL 62321-001

Literary Exploration continuted

The Fascinating World of— Bats by Angels Julivert
A First Look at Bats by Millicent E. Selsam
I Can Read About Bats by Elizabeth Warren
Loose Tooth by Steven Kroll
Shadows of Night: The Hidden World of the Little Brown Bat by Barbara
    Bash
StellaLuna by Janell Cannon

Language Experience

• How many words can your students come up with that rhyme with
  the word *bat*?

• Create a Venn diagram depicting the similarities and differences
  between a bat and a cat.

TLC10454 Copyright © Teaching & Learning Company, Carthage, IL 62321-0010

Science/Health Experience

- Today is a good day to study the science of bats and their habitat.

Social Studies Experience

- Learn about areas of the world where bats are prevalent.

Music/Dramatic Experience

- Borrow a *Batman* soundtrack from your local library to play quietly in the background while students work on their projects.

Physical/Sensory Experience

- After teaching about echolocation (which helps bats avoid bumping into things, even with their poor eyesight), let younger students "fly" around the room like bats.

TLC10454 Copyright © Teaching & Learning Company, Carthage, IL 62321-001

Arts/Crafts Experience

• Let students cut out bat shapes from black construction paper, then stick on white reinforcement rings for eyes, and suspend them from your classroom ceiling.

Follow-Up/Homework Idea

• B is for bat. Challenge students to make a list of things they find at home that start with the letter "B."

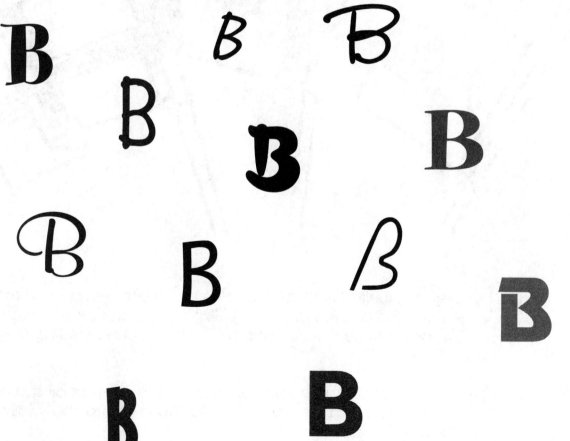

Goin' "Batty"

Goin' "Batty"

Goin' "Batty"

United
Nations

United
Nations

United
Nations

United Nations Day

October 24

Setting the Stage

- Set up your classroom as a mini United Nations today with students representing different countries. Have each student make a different country's flag and attach to a craft stick or straw. Stick the flag in clay and display it at his or her desk throughout the day.

- Display a United Nations flag (blue and white with a world map surrounded by olive branches). Explain that the olive branches symbolize peace. Add related literature around the flag to gather interest.

- Display pictures of people from around the world against a backdrop of a rainbow with the caption: "Our World Is a Rainbow Full of Beautiful People!"

TLC10454 Copyright © Teaching & Learning Company, Carthage, IL 62321-0010

Historical Background

This day is set aside to honor the United Nations organization, which promotes peace and human rights. The United Nations was founded on this day in 1945.

Literary Exploration

People by Peter Spier
The Story of the United Nations by R. Conrad Stein
This Is the United Nations by Miroslav Sasek
The United Nations by Stewart Ross
The United Nations by Harold Woods
The United Nations by Adam Woog
The United Nations from A to Z by Nancy Winslow Parker

Writing Experience

• Encourage students to write about a world problem they would like the United Nations to address at their next meeting. They may include their own suggestions for solving the problem. See reproducible on page 135.

a Letter to the UNITED NATIONS...

Signed: _____

United
Nations

United
Nations

United
Nations

Math Experience

- Play Around the World Math! One student stands behind another student seated at a desk. When the teacher calls out a math review problem, both students try to say the answer first. The one who says the correct answer first gets to move to the next desk. The student who was second sits down at the first desk. The aim is for the student to go "around the world" of desks before they have to sit down.

- Review the basics of the metric system, which is the international system of measurement.

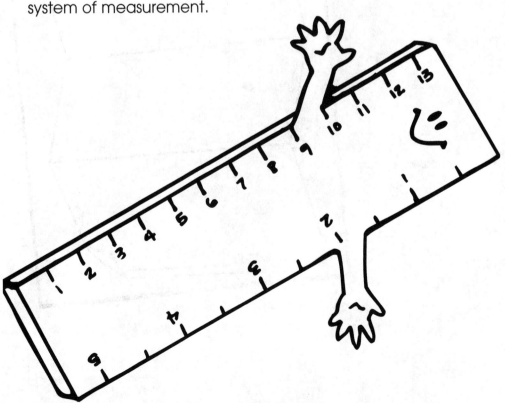

TLC10454 Copyright © Teaching & Learning Company, Carthage, IL 62321-0010

Social Studies Experience

• If you set up your room as a mini United Nations, let students learn more about their selected countries and share the information with the rest of the class.

Music/Dramatic Experience

• Sing the children's favorite, "It's a Small World" (words and music by Richard Sherman).

Physical/Sensory Experience

• Play some international games such as jump rope, hopscotch and tag.

Arts/Crafts Experience

• Students will enjoy making a paper doll chain of children from around the world. After fan folding a large piece of white paper lengthwise, cut the figure of a person against the fold and then open to reveal paper cut-outs.

United Nations

United Nations

United Nations

Extension Activities

- Challenge students to gather donations from local community members to send to the UNICEF fund for children all over the world.

- Invite visitors from other countries to come and share information or memorabilia from their respective countries with your class.

Values Education Experience

- Discuss the value of peace and cooperation among individuals to bring about global peace. Talk about mutual tolerance, understanding and appreciating cultures around the world.

Follow-Up/Homework Idea

- Encourage students to begin making their own homes more peaceful by honoring everyone's rights as family members.

TLC10454 Copyright © Teaching & Learning Company, Carthage, IL 62321-0010

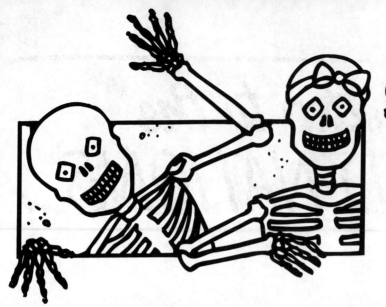

Skeleton and Skills Day

October 25

Setting the Stage

- "I can feel it in my bones." Take advantage of children's natural fascination with skeletons to intoduce some fascinating facts.

- Display pictures, magazines and books related to the skeletal system. See if you can get any discarded X-rays from a local hospital to use in the display. A local butcher or high school biology department may be willing to give you bones you can use in your display.

- Display humorous stories around a skeleton with the caption: "Stories to Tickle Your Funny Bone!"

- Construct a semantic map or web listing the facts students know (or would like to know) about human bones.

Literary Exploration

Blood and Guts: A Working Guide to Your Own Insides by Linda Allison
The Bones Book & Skeletons by Stephen Cumbaa
The Book About Your Skeleton by Ruth Belov Gross
Cuts, Breaks, Bruises and Burns by Joanna Cole
Funnybones by Janet and Allan Ahlberg
Hob Goblin and the Skeleton by Alice Schertle
Incredible Skeleton Secrets by Angela Wilkes
Inspector Bodyguard Patrols the Land of U by Vicki Cobb

TLC10454 Copyright © Teaching & Learning Company, Carthage, IL 62321-0010

Literary Exploration continued

Blood and Guts: A Working Guide to Your Own Insides by Linda Allison
The Bones Book & Skeletons by Stephen Cumbaa
The Book About Your Skeleton by Ruth Belov Gross
Cuts, Breaks, Bruises and Burns by Joanna Cole
Funnybones by Janet and Allan Ahlberg
Hob Goblin and the Skeleton by Alice Schertle
Incredible Skeleton Secrets by Angela Wilkes
Inspector Bodyguard Patrols the Land of U by Vicki Cobb
Magic School Bus Inside the Human Body by Joanna Cole
Movement by John Gaskin
The Skeleton and Movement by Brian Ward
Skeleton Crew by Allan Ahlberg
The Skeleton Inside You by Paul Showers
Skeleton Parade by Jack Prelutsky
Skeletons: An Inside Book About Animals by Jinny Johnson
Skeletons! Skeletons! All About Bones by Katy Hall
Skeletons That Fit by Margaret W. Merrill
Them Bones by Ian Dicks
What to Do When Your Mom or Dad Says, "Stand Up Straight" by Joy Berry
Your Skeleton and Skin by Ray Broekel

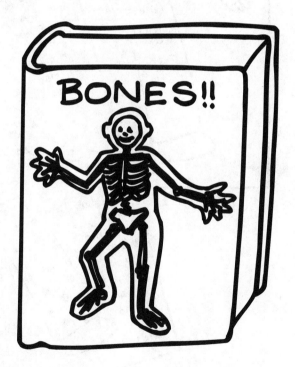

Language Experience

- Create a class Venn diagram depicting the similarities and differences between bones and teeth.

TLC10454 Copyright © Teaching & Learning Company, Carthage, IL 62321-0010

Writing Experience

- Give students the bone patterns on page 142 to write "stories to tickle your funny bone!"

- Use the body outline on page 143 to encourage students to write "All About Me" shape books. (These can be great decorations for Parent/Teacher Night.)

- Students can also use the body outline to write an "About Me" poem with the letters in their name.

Cute
Agile
Reader
Stylish
Observant
Nice

My name is Jessica Ann. I am 9 years old. I live with my family San Jose. I like to study science, art, and math.

I also play the piano and like to practice early in the morning before I go to school. My favorite food to eat is pizza.

My favorite activity is to visit the art museum and the zoo with my family. We go often together.

I like to go camping by a lake. My dad has taught me to fish. We like to cook them for dinner.

Math Experience

- The longest bone in our bodies is the femur, the thigh bone in the leg; the smallest is the stapes, the stirrup-shaped bone in the ears. Have students measure some of the more prominent bones in their bodies.

TLC10454 Copyright © Teaching & Learning Company, Carthage, IL 62321-0010

Science/Health Experience

• Cut some bones in half and let students examine them with magnifying glasses. Help them identify the cartilage, the shaft and bone marrow. If you are not able to get larger bones, a stewed chicken (that hasn't been boiled too long) can be deboned. Set aside a few of the bones to be put in a vinegar solution for observation over the next week or so. The acid in the vinegar will dissolve the minerals in the bones, causing them to grow soft and bendable. Students will be interested to find out what happens when a bone is soaked in a cola drink for a few days.

• Babies are born with about 300 bones. As they grow, some of these bones fuse together (such as the "soft spot" on the head) and by adulthood, they only have about 206 bones. Bones hold our bodies up (acting as a frame) and give them structure. Illustrate this with a coat hanger, showing how it provides a "skeletal" framework for our clothes.

• Let students research foods in our diets that are rich in calcium and phosphorus. Discuss our need for these minerals and the importance of exercise to keep bones strong and help guard against bone disease.

• Illustrate how joints move and work. Show how a metal hinge joint, or two toilet paper tubes taped together at one end, allows movement in a given direction. Demonstrate how a pivot joint (such as in a gooseneck lamp) allows us to turn our head. Use a pencil sharpener to show how a ball-and-socket joint, found in our hips and shoulders, allows limited movement in all directions.

Social Studies Experience

• Have your students ever heard the expression, "a bone to pick" with someone? Discuss what it means, then emphasize the importance of peaceful resolution in any difficulty with another person.

Music/Dramatic Experience

• Sing the old classic, "Dem Bones," with your class.

Dem Bones

(Chorus)
"Dem bones, dem bones, dem dry bones,
Dem bones, dem bones, dem dry bone,
Dem bones, dem bones, dem dry bones,
Dem bones, dem bones, dem bones.

The toe bone's connected to the foot bone,
The foot bone's connected to the ankle bone."
(Continue progressing up the body.)

Physical/Sensory Experience

• Play Simon Says using major bone areas. Simon says, "Touch your elbow."

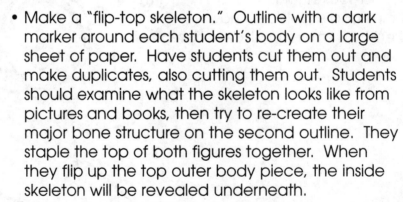

Arts/Crafts Experience

• Let students construct skeletons from cut-apart drinking straws.

• Make a "flip-top skeleton." Outline with a dark marker around each student's body on a large sheet of paper. Have students cut them out and make duplicates, also cutting them out. Students should examine what the skeleton looks like from pictures and books, then try to re-create their major bone structure on the second outline. They staple the top of both figures together. When they flip up the top outer body piece, the inside skeleton will be revealed underneath.

• Let students create paper plate skeletons that can be hung around the room. Brad fasteners can be used to hold bones together and make the skeletons moveable! Each skeleton requires nine paper plates and 15 brad fasteners. See patterns on pages 144-147.

• Search "Milk Jug Skeleton" on the internet to find the pattern and directions for constructing a skeleton of plastic milk jugs.

TLC10454 Copyright © Teaching & Learning Company, Carthage, IL 62321-0010

Extension Activities

- Invite an X-ray technician to visit your class and talk about bones.

- Invite a doctor to visit your class to explain how to tell if a bone is broken, and how a cast is made for the broken area. Some precautionary advice about how to keep from breaking bones would also be helpful.

- Take a trip to a hospital X-ray department to see X rays depicting bones that are broken and intact.

- Make Edible Bones for a snack! Mix up your favorite sugar cookie recipe according to the directions. Shape the dough into bones. Bake at 300°F for about 20 minutes or until they're lightly browned. Cool and serve.

TLC10454 Copyright © Teaching & Learning Company, Carthage, IL 62321-0010

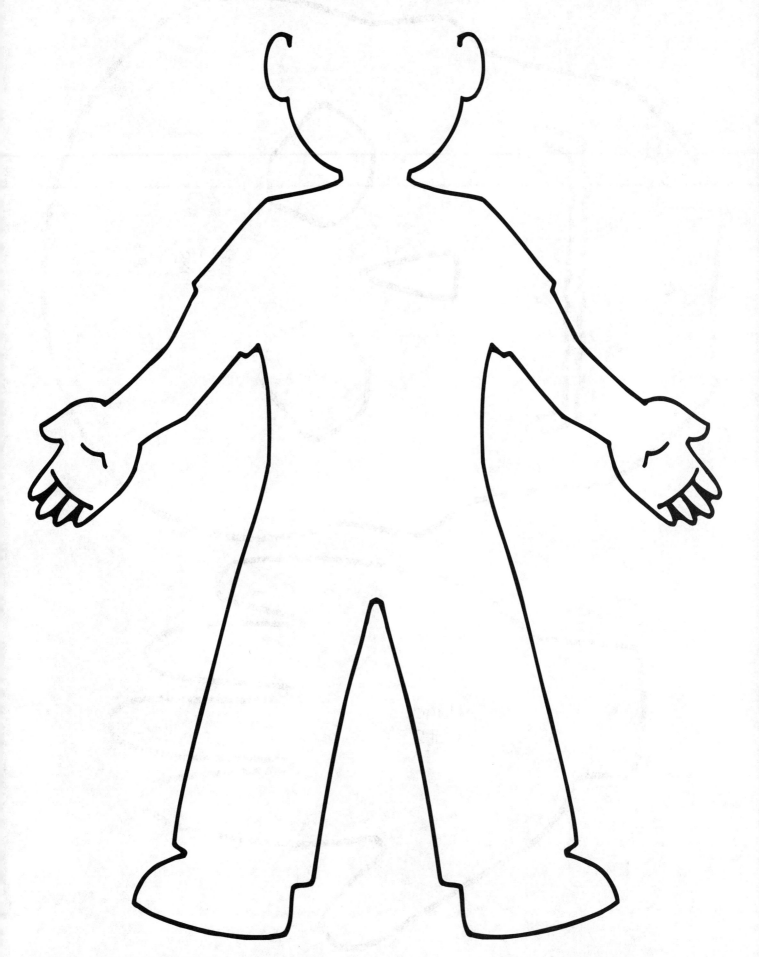

TLC10454 Copyright © Teaching & Learning Company, Carthage, IL 62321-0010

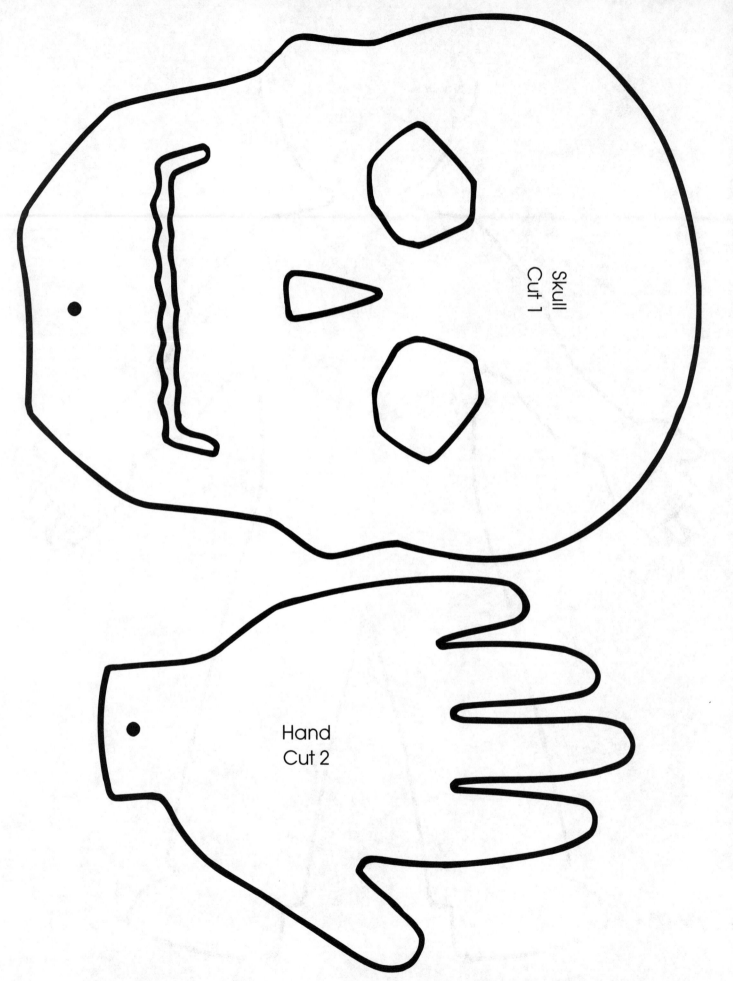

Skull
Cut 1

Hand
Cut 2

TLC10454 Copyright © Teaching & Learning Company, Carthage, IL 62321-0010

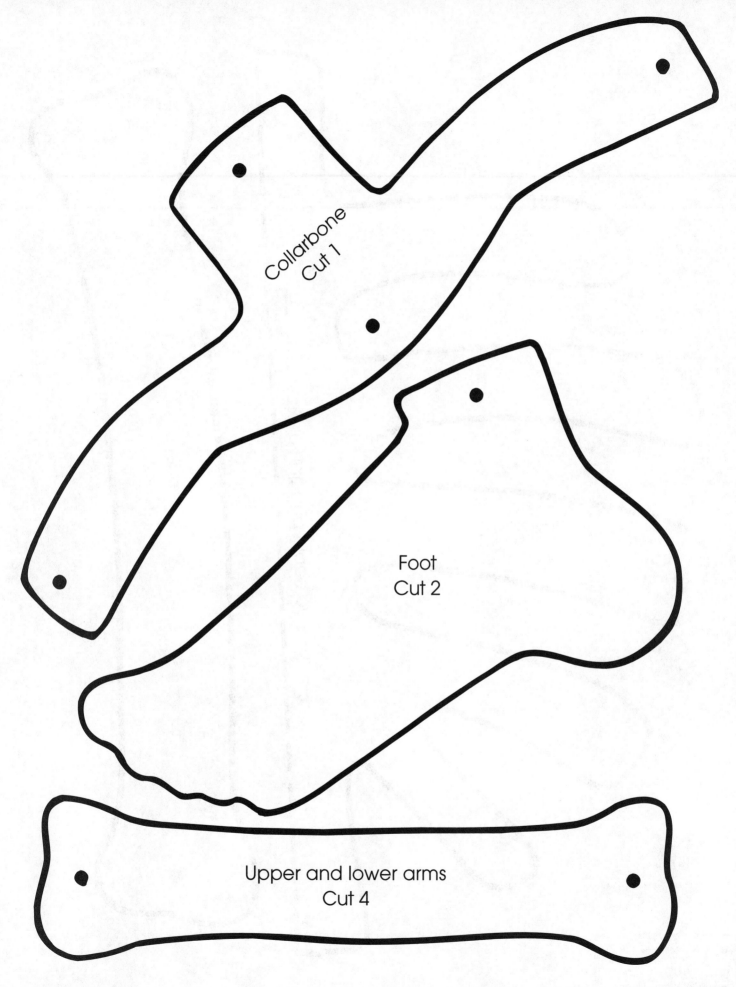

Collarbone
Cut 1

Foot
Cut 2

Upper and lower arms
Cut 4

TLC10454 Copyright © Teaching & Learning Company, Carthage, IL 62321-0010

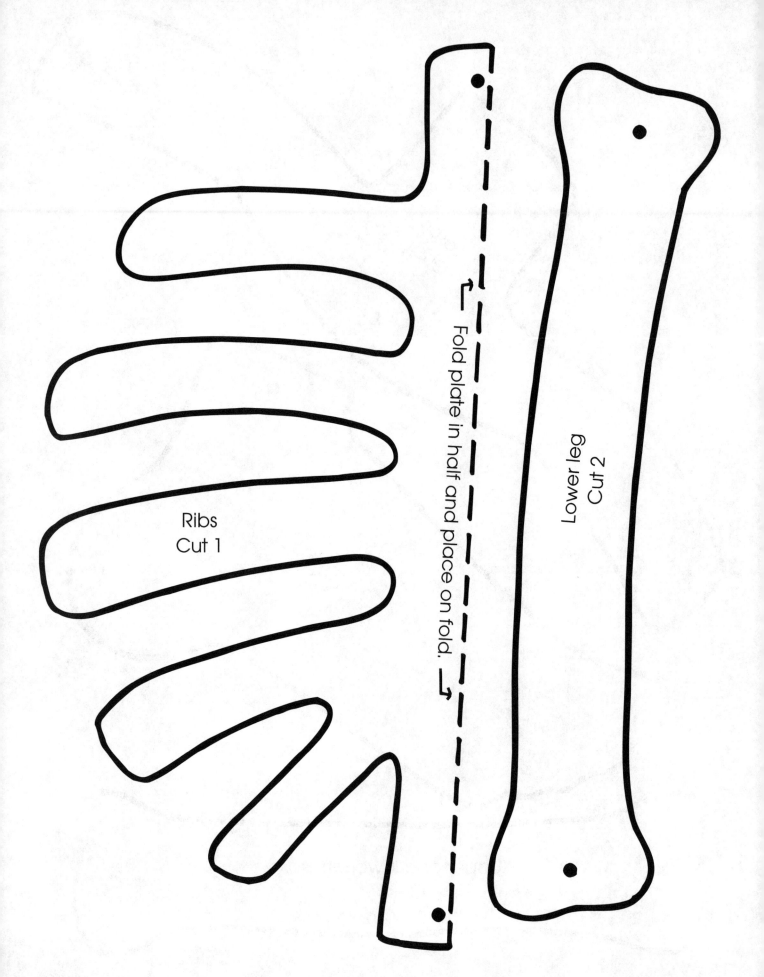

Ribs
Cut 1

Fold plate in half and place on fold.

Lower leg
Cut 2

146

TLC10454 Copyright © Teaching & Learning Company, Carthage, IL 62321-0010

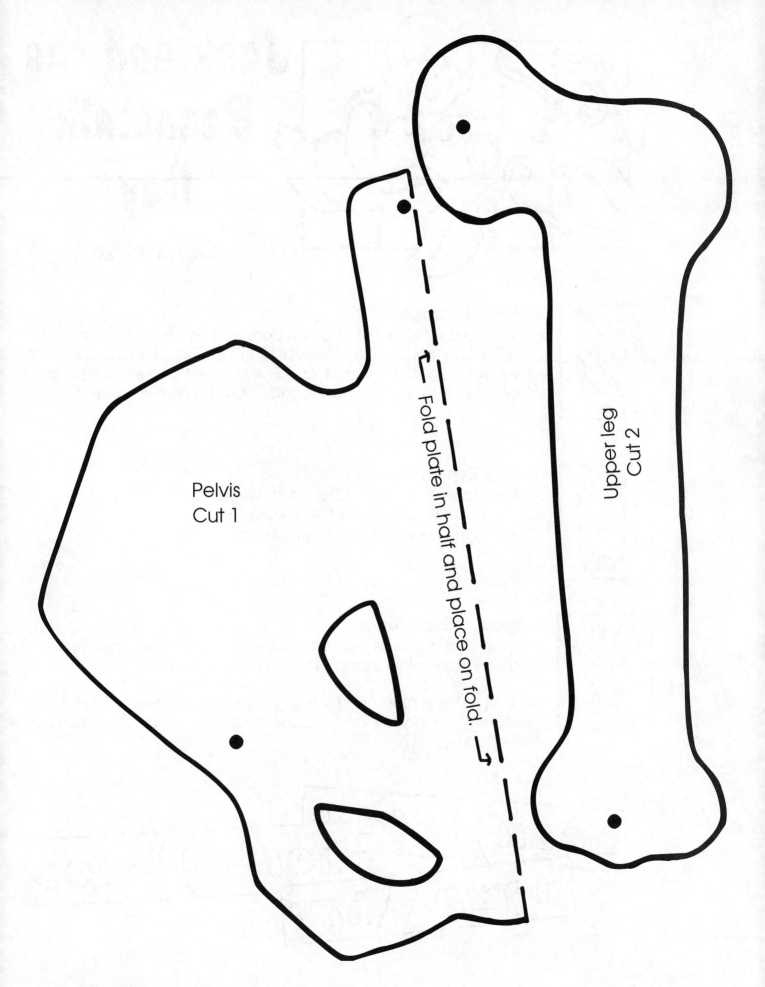

Pelvis
Cut 1

Fold plate in half and place on fold.

Upper leg
Cut 2

TLC10454 Copyright © Teaching & Learning Company, Carthage, IL 62321-0010

Jack and the Beanstalk Day

October 26

Setting the Stage
- Create a beanstalk out of green construction paper that runs from the floor up the length of the wall to the ceiling. Add clouds made from cotton batting at the top. Green leaves or green crepe paper that can be loosely braided together adds a nice 3-D effect!

Literary Exploration
Jack and the Beanstalk by Carol Ottolenghi
Jack and the Beanstalk by Steven Kellogg
Jack and the Beanstalk by Maggie Moore

Language Experience
- Explain that the word *beanstalk* is a compound word. Brainstorm as a class as many other compound words they can.

- Create a Venn diagram depicting the similarities and differences between a beanstalk and a ladder (the usual mode of climbing up to reach something).

TLC10454 Copyright © Teaching & Learning Company, Carthage, IL 62321-0010

Writing Experience

• Allow students the opportunity to write about a situation in the story "Jack and the Beanstalk" from either Jack's or the giant's point of view. See reproducible on page 151.

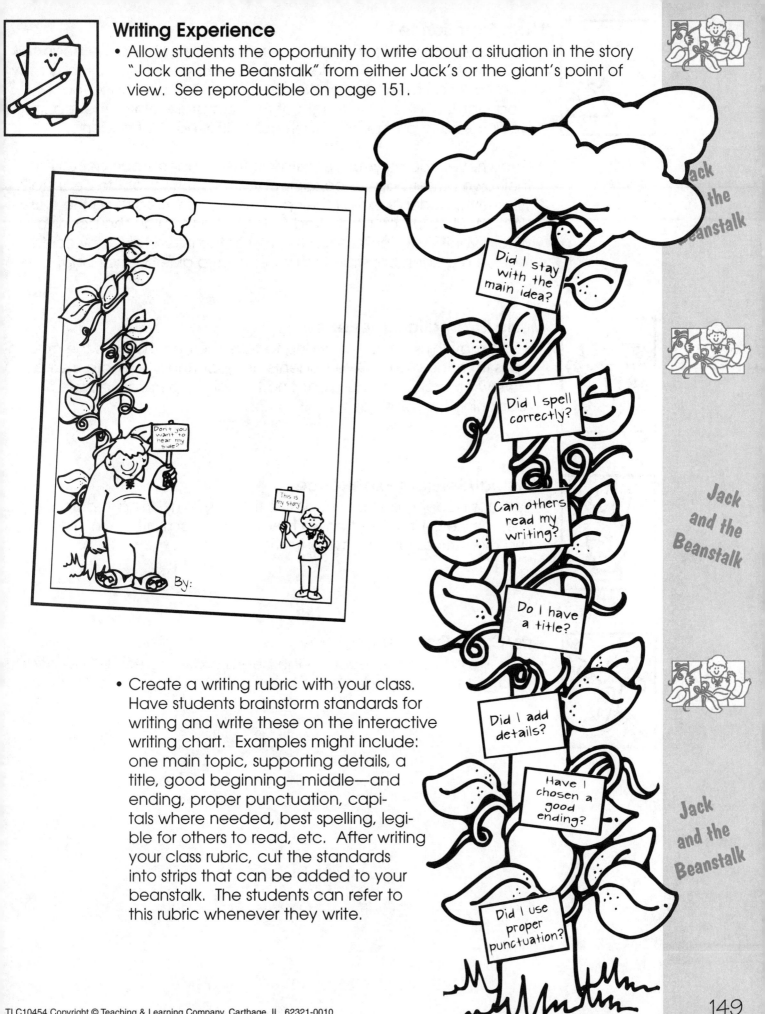

Don't you want to hear my side?

This is my story

By:

Did I stay with the main idea?

Did I spell correctly?

Can others read my writing?

Do I have a title?

Did I add details?

Have I chosen a good ending?

Did I use proper punctuation?

• Create a writing rubric with your class. Have students brainstorm standards for writing and write these on the interactive writing chart. Examples might include: one main topic, supporting details, a title, good beginning—middle—and ending, proper punctuation, capitals where needed, best spelling, legible for others to read, etc. After writing your class rubric, cut the standards into strips that can be added to your beanstalk. The students can refer to this rubric whenever they write.

Math Experience

- Using a yardstick, allow students to measure lengths up the beanstalk. Measurements can be made in inches, feet, yards, etc. Or they may want to try an exercise in metric measuring. They can label each measurement along the length of the beanstalk. Note: The teacher would need to put up any labels out of the reach of students.

- If you have labeled your beanstalk in feet, students can decorate their own paper bags to be secured at the bottom of the beanstalk. Whenever students exhibit their proficiency as writers using the class rubric, their bag can be moved (a foot at a time) up the beanstalk. Whenever the students reach the top of the beanstalk, they could receive a golden construction paper egg to glue on their bag.

Music/Dramatic Experience

- Some may think Jack was wrong to take the hen that lays the golden eggs from the giant. Give students an opportunity to share their point of view as Jack or as the giant and to make a persuasive case supporting their position.

Physical/Sensory Experience

- Perhaps students can beef up their fitness skills (running in place, stretches, etc.) in order to help them be physically fit just in case they find themselves running away from a giant.

Arts/Crafts Experience

- Students could help decorate the beanstalk with green leaves or add gold glitter to the golden eggs to be put at the top of the beanstalk.

TLC10454 Copyright © Teaching & Learning Company, Carthage, IL 62321-0010

By:

Teddy Roosevelt's Birthday

October 27

Setting the Stage

• Display a teddy bear with books that deal with Theodore Roosevelt, nature or conservation.

• Construct a semantic web with facts your students know (or would like to know) about conservation.

Historical Background

Theodore "Teddy" Roosevelt was the 26th President of the United States. He was born on this date in 1858.

Literary Exploration

Bully for You, Theodore Roosevelt! by Jean Fritz
The First Teddy Bear by Helen Kay
Theodore Roosevelt: All Around Boy by Edd Winfield Parks
Theodore Roosevelt and the Rough Riders by Henry Castor
Theodore Roosevelt: Rough Rider by Louis Sabin
Theodore Roosevelt: Young Rough Rider by Edd Winfield Parks

TLC10454 Copyright © Teaching & Learning Company, Carthage, IL 62321-0010

Language Experience

Encourage students to brainstorm words they can think of that rhyme with *Teddy*.

Science/Health Experience

• Research and discuss Roosevelt's conservation efforts.

Social Studies Experience

• Encourage interested students to research Teddy Roosevelt or the Spanish-American War (in which he led a volunteer fighting group known as the Rough Riders). Give them an opportunity to share their findings with the rest of the class.

Physical/Sensory Experience

• Weak from childhood illnesses, Teddy Roosevelt worked hard to build and maintain a strong and healthy body. Spend a few minutes doing some basic fitness exercises such as jumping jacks or sit-ups.

Extension Activities

- President Roosevelt received the Nobel Peace Prize for his work with conservation. Have students brainstorm some conservation ideas to help in areas around your school. Hand out mock prizes to those who go the "extra mile." See reproducibles on page 155.

Values Education Experience

- Explain how the Teddy bear got its name. During a hunting trip, according to some versions of the story, Roosevelt found a bear cub near his tent. While his hunting companions reached for their guns, Roosevelt stood alone in his desire to leave the cub unharmed and untouched. A national cartoonist (Clifford Berryman) drew a picture of the incident, which became very popular. Not long afterward, a candy store owner called the stuffed animal toys in his window display, "Teddy's Bears." About a year later, he closed the candy store and founded the Ideal Novelty and Toy Company! Lead a discussion on standing up for what you believe, even if you are all alone.

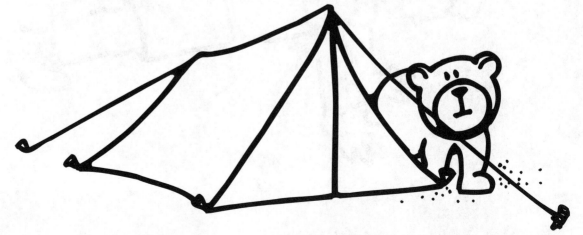

TLC10454 Copyright © Teaching & Learning Company, Carthage, IL 62321-0010

NOBEL
Peace Prize

To: _____

For: _____

_____

_____

NOBEL
Peace Prize

To: _____

For: _____

_____

_____

NOBEL
Peace Prize

To: _____

For: _____

_____

_____

NOBEL
Peace Prize

To: _____

For: _____

_____

_____

TLC10454 Copyright © Teaching & Learning Company, Carthage, IL 62321-0010

Spindly Spider Day

October 28

Setting the Stage

• Capitalize on students' natural fascination with creepy, crawly things—spiders! (Some children may be genuinely afraid of even "toy" spiders. Please guide your use of these activities according to your class' temperment and encourage all students to respect one another.)

• Display spider pictures from magazines and spider-related literature to gather excitement about today's activities.

• Novelty stores sell mock spiderwebs at this time of year. Black yarn or thread can also be substituted. Make spiderwebs in any corner of the room and suspend them from the ceiling. Add student-made spiders among the web sections and hang others from the ceiling in varying lengths. Hang some with elastic so they bounce.

• Construct a semantic map or "web" with all the facts your students know (or would like to know) about spiders.

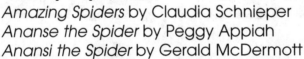

Literary Exploration

Amazing Spiders by Claudia Schnieper
Ananse the Spider by Peggy Appiah
Anansi the Spider by Gerald McDermott
Aranea: A Story About a Spider by Jenny Wagner
Be Nice to Spiders by Margaret Graham
Black Widow Spiders by Louise Martin
Charlotte's Web by E.B. White
Clovis Crawfish and the Spinning Spider by Mary Alice Fontenot
Dance, Spider, Dance! by Robert Krauss
Discovering Spiders by Malcolm Penny
Eency Weency Spider by Joanne Oppenheim
Extremely Weird Spiders by Sarah Lovelett
A First Look at Spiders by Millicent Ellis Selsam
First Sight Spiders by Lionel Bender
Fishing Spiders by Louise Martin
Funnel Web Spiders by Louise Martin
Itsy Bitsy Spider by Dianne O'Quinn Burke
The Itsy Bitsy Spider by Iza Trapani

TLC10454 Copyright © Teaching & Learning Company, Carthage, IL 62321-0010

Literary Exploration continued

The Lady and the Spider by Faith McNulty
The Life Cycle of a Spider by Jill Bailey
101 Wacky Facts About Bugs and Spiders by Jean Waricha
The Roly Poly Spider by Jill Sardegna
Rosie Sips Spiders by Alison Lester
Someone Saw a Spider by Shirley Climo
Songs About Insects, Bugs and Squiggley Things by Jane Lawliss Murphy
Spider by Michael Chinery
Spider (series) by Robert Krauss
A Spider and a Pig by Carol Morley
Spider in the Sky by Anne Rose
Spider on the Floor by Bill Russell
Spider Silk by A. Golden
Spiders by Donna Bailey
Spiders by Norman Barrett
Spiders by Lillian Bason
Spiders by Timothy Biel
Spiders by Jane Dallinger
Spiders by Gail Gibbons
Spiders by David Hawcock
Spiders by Bill Ivey
Spiders by Terry Jennings
The Spiders by Margaret Lane
Spiders by Dean Morris
Spiders by Alexandra Parsons
Spiders by Kate Petty
Spiders by Ralph Whitlock
Spiders Are Animals by Holloway and Harper
Spiders in the Fruit Cellar by B.M. Joose
Spider's Lunch by Joanna Cole
Spider's Web by Christine Back
Spider Watching by Vivian French
Spider Watching by David Webster
The Story of Spiders by Dorothy Edwards Shuttlesworth
Tarantula Spiders by Louise Martin
Trap Door Spiders by Louise Martin
The Very Busy Spider by Eric Carle
Zoe's Webs by T. West

Spindly Spider

Spindly Spider

Spindly Spider

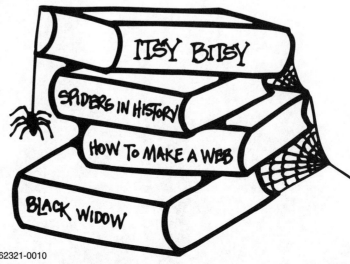

Language Experience

- Challenge students to read *101 Wacky Facts About Bugs and Spiders* by Jean Waricha, then try to stump the class with some of the amazing spider facts.

- Using the reproducible on page 163, have students write words in the web to describe spiders.

Spiders are...

- Create a class Venn diagram with the similarities and differences between a spider and an insect.

TLC10454 Copyright © Teaching & Learning Company, Carthage, IL 62321-0010

Writing Experience

- Invite students to write descriptions of spiderwebs. For a writing border, let each student press a finger on an inkpad, then make "fingerprint" spiders around the edge of the page. They'll need to draw eight legs on each spider.

Math Experience

- How about doing some "Spidery Sums"? Draw some spiderwebs on the board, allowing a little space between each web section to write numbers. In the middle of the web, write a number. Have students work in cooperative groups to come up with addends that fit that particular sum. Example: If a 9 were in the center of the web, students might write 6 + 3 or 5 + 4 or 3 x 3 in the web.

- Spiders just don't seem to sit still! Review subtraction skills with spider stories. In each story problem, a certain number of spiders wander away). For younger students, use small plastic spiders (found in novelty stores) as math manipulatives. See patterns on page 164.

Science/Health Experience

- Study the science of spiders and their habitats.

- Review spider safety. Most spiders are harmless, but there are a few (such as Black Widow or Brown Recluse) that students need to take precautionary measures with if they see them.

TLC10454 Copyright © Teaching & Learning Company, Carthage, IL 62321-0010

Social Studies Experience

- In ancient times, some people thought spiders had curative powers. People would swallow a spider (like a pill) to cure an illness. Some even carried a spider in a nutshell around the neck for emergency treatment for fevers or as a dressing for wounds.

Music/Dramatic Experience

- Younger students will enjoy singing the classic, "Itsy Bitsy Spider."

- Let students act out a dramatic version of "Little Miss Muffet."

Physical/Sensory Experience

- Take time for a nature walk to hunt for spiders and spiderwebs. If possible, take magnifying glasses for students to use. If you find spiders, make temporary homes for them in jars with air holes punched in the lids. Each jar can have a wet sponge on the bottom for moisture with grass, leaves or twigs to simulate a natural habitat. Watch to see if the spiders begin to spin webs inside their jars.

- Play a game of Step into My Parlor, Said the Spider to the Fly. Choose a student to be the "spider" in the "web" (the middle of the playing area). Other students are flies around the spider. The spider chants, "Step into My Parlor, Said the Spider to the Fly" and the flies try to get closer and closer to the spider without getting caught. When the spider yells, "Trapped!" he tries to catch any nearby flies. Flies that are caught become spiders also until there are no more flies.

160

Arts/Crafts Experience

• Students can make simple black spiders by cutting black circles and attaching black strips for legs. The legs can be accordion-folded to make the spider appear to be standing up. Add construction paper or wiggly craft eyes. See patterns on pages 165 and 166.

• Hand out spiderweb patterns. Students place clear plastic wrap over the pattern and draw a continuing line of glue over the entire pattern. After they dry they can be carefully lifted off. The glue web can be mounted on dark construction paper for a beautiful web. Add glitter glue for a "dew-like" effect on the web. See reproducible on page 167.

• Give each student a small dab of black tempera paint and a cotton swab. The students fan out the black paint with the swab to make eight legs on the black spider.

• Large black buttons (with four holes) can be made into spiders. Thread black pipe cleaners into the holes and bend them to resemble eight legs. Position the legs to support the spider body. Glue on wiggly craft eyes to the top of the button to create the face.

• Make "spaghetti webs." Cook spaghetti noodles according to the package directions. Drain the spaghetti and set it aside to cool. Mix glue and water, a half and half mixture. Students then dip the cooked spaghetti in the glue mixture and arrange it into a web. Yarn can be substituted for spaghetti.

Extension Activities

• Some museums offer spider displays in glass cases. Take your students to observe any in your area and encourage them to make observational drawings.

• Make these scary spider treats:

Wrinkly Grandfather Spiders
Have students stick pretzel stick legs into a large soft prune.

Cookie Spider
Add black licorice legs to a chocolate sandwich cookie. Students can use a little of the white icing from inside the cookie to attach two Red Hot "eyes" to the top of the cookie.

Chinese Noodle Spider
Let students stick eight crunchy Chinese noodles into a large marshmallow "body." Melt chocolate chips and spoon them over the "spider body."

TLC10454 Copyright © Teaching & Learning Company, Carthage, IL 62321-001

TLC10454 Copyright © Teaching & Learning Company, Carthage, IL 62321-0010

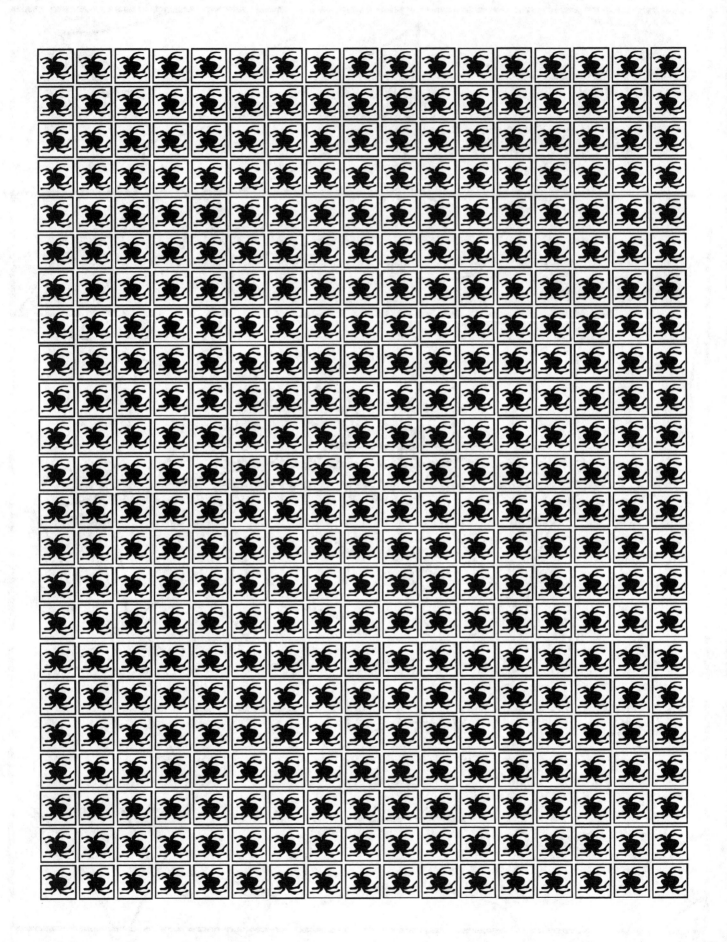

164

TLC10454 Copyright © Teaching & Learning Company, Carthage, IL 62321-0010

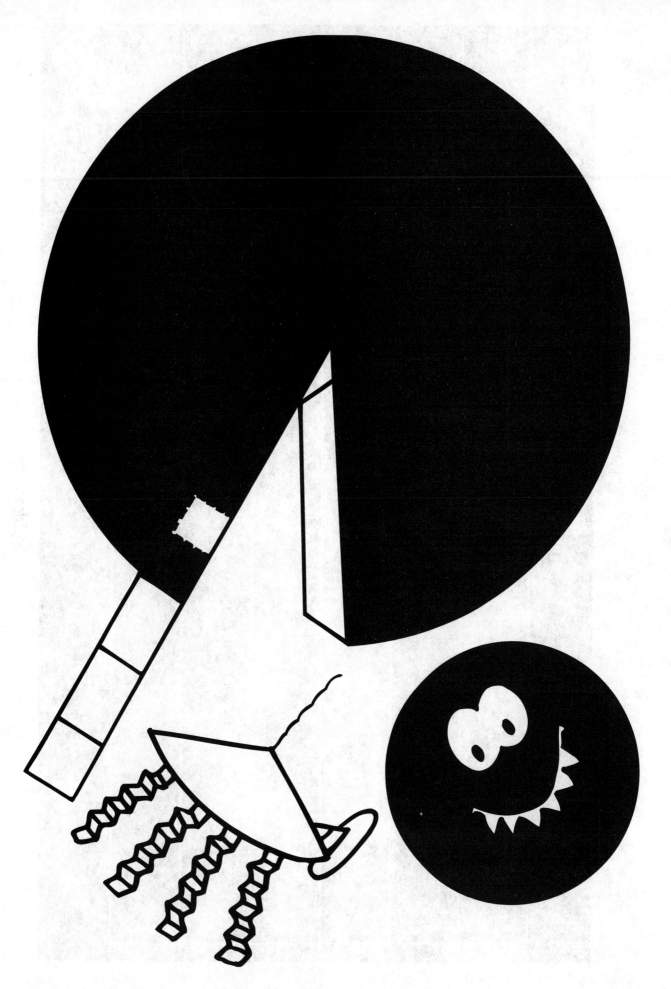

Spider Legs

166

TLC10454 Copyright © Teaching & Learning Company, Carthage, IL 62321-001

TLC10454 Copyright © Teaching & Learning Company, Carthage, IL 62321-0010

Make-Believe Day

October 29

Setting the Stage

- Display a spooky background (yellow moon with a black silhouette of a cat against it, with pumpkins sitting on top of a white picket fence). Use it to display student work.

- At this time of year, many students are getting excited about Halloween. Many are contemplating now they are going to dress for Halloween trick-or-treating. Younger children are often scared as well as intrigued by masks, decorations and events such as haunted houses. If children are frightened by masks, suggest some face painting instead. Use Make-Believe Day to stress the silliness of Halloween, avoiding the sometimes-gory elements. Encourage students to have fun as they pretend and "make-believe" today!

Literary Exploration

Ellen Tebbits by Beverly Cleary
The Most Awful Play by Patricia Reilly Giff
The One in the Middle Is a Green Kangaroo by Judy Blume
The Pudgy Book of Make-Believe by Andrea Brooks
The Tall Book of Make-Believe by Jane Werner
When Monsters Seem Real by Fred Rogers

TLC10454 Copyright © Teaching & Learning Company, Carthage, IL 62321-0010

Language Experience
• Let students brainstorm every make-believe costume they can think of, then list them in alphabetical order.

• Let students work on their oral language skills by playing this "Knock-Knock" game in pairs. One student closes his eyes and turns his back to his partner. The other student "knocks" gently on his "door" (back). The first student asks, "Who is it?" The other student describes what he looks like in an imaginary costume until the first student guesses "who" or what his partner is.

      Example:

"Knock, Knock"
"Who Is It?"
"I have a
long, fancy dress.
I wear a crown with sparkles!"
"Oh, you're a princess!"

Writing Experience
• Encourage students to write about what they like to pretend.

Math Experience
• Students will enjoy taking a survey of other students' favorite fantasy characters. This information can be added to a class bar graph.

Social Studies Experience
• Let interested students research what other countries do for Halloween.

• Many countries traditionally make and wear masks (Native Americans and Eskimo tribal masks, African ceremonial masks).

• If appropriate, give students an opportunity to verbalize their feelings about Halloween. Sometimes they are frightened about the things they see and aren't aware that other children share the same fears. Talk about ways they can deal with their feelings and enjoy the holiday.

TLC10454 Copyright © Teaching & Learning Company, Carthage, IL 62321-0010

Music/Dramatic Experience

• Borrow Linda Arnold's "Make-Believe" (sound recording) from a local library.

Physical/Sensory Experience

• Let students parade around the room pretending they have a costume on. Explain that the way they walk or present themselves as a character lends a lot to its believability. For example, Frankenstein would have heavy, rigid movements, but a ballerina would walk very lightly and delicately.

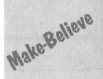

Arts/Crafts Experience

- Students will enjoy drawing a picture, pressing heavily with their crayons. Then have them wash a layer of black paint over it for a "spooky" effect!

Values Education Experience

- Discuss the value of imagination, which allows us to explore infinite possibilities!

TLC10454 Copyright © Teaching & Learning Company, Carthage, IL 62321-0010

Great Pumpkin Day

October 30

Setting the Stage

- Display large and small pumpkins (or oranges decorated like pumpkins with jack-o'-lantern faces) to gather excitement in the day. Students can make a scarecrow using a pumpkin as the head.

- Create a semantic web with facts your students know (or want to know) about pumpkins to help plan your day's activities.

Historical Background

In the Charles M. Schulz' *Peanuts* cartoon series, Linus can be found on the eve of Halloween waiting patiently all night for the appearance of the "Great Pumpkin" who, according to legend, brings treats for all good boys and girls.

TLC10454 Copyright © Teaching & Learning Company, Carthage, IL 62321-0010

Literary Exploration

The All-Around Pumpkin Book by Margery Cuyler
Apples and Pumpkins by Anne Rockwell
The Biggest Pumpkin Ever by Steven Kroll
Big Pumpkin by Erica Silverman
The Great Pumpkin Switch by Megan McDonald
In a Pumpkin Shell: A Mother Goose ABC by Mother Goose
It's Pumpkin Time! by Zoe Hall
It's the Great Pumpkin, Charlie Brown by Charles M. Schulz
Jeb Scarecrow's Pumpkin Patch by Jana Dillion
The Magic Pumpkin by Bill Martin
The Magic Pumpkin by Lucille Setle
The Magic Pumpkin by Gloria Skurzynski
The Mystery of the Flying Orange Pumpkin by Steven Kellogg
Patchy Pumpkin Finds Himself a Home! by Sandy Lardinois
The Perky Little Pumpkin by Margaret Friskey
The Pumpkin Blanket by Debora Turney Zagwyn
Pumpkin Giant by Mary Wilkins
Pumpkin Light by David Ray
Pumpkin Moonshine by Tasha Tudor
The Pumpkin Patch by Elizabeth King
Pumpkin Time by Jan Andrews
Pumpkin, Pumpkin by Jeanne Titherington
Pumpkins: A Story for a Field by Mary Lyn Ray
Sir William and the Pumpkin Monster by Margery Cuyler
The Vanishing Pumpkin by Tony Johnston
Wonderful Pumpkin by Lennart Hellsing

TLC10454 Copyright © Teaching & Learning Company, Carthage, IL 62321-0010

Language Experience

• Students can create a class Venn diagram depicting the similarities and differences between a pumpkin and a jack-o'-lantern.

Writing Experience

• Have students write the sequential steps in carving a pumpkin into a jack-o'-lantern. See reproducible on page 181.

HOW TO CARVE A
JACK-O-LANTERN

Name:_____

TLC10454 Copyright © Teaching & Learning Company, Carthage, IL 62321-0010

175

Great
Pumpkin

Great
Pumpkin

Great
Pumpkin

Math Experience

• How about a little pumpkin math? Invite students to bring small pumpkins from home. They can measure the weight and circumference of pumpkins, after estimating them. Let them weigh pumpkins with, then without seeds. They can estimate, then count the number of seeds.

A class graph can be made with seeds from individual pumpkins.

Science/Health Experience

• This would be a good opportunity to review kitchen tool safety if your class is involved with pumpkin carving today.

• Students will enjoy learning how pumpkins grow from seed to harvest and what they need in order to grow.

176

TLC10454 Copyright © Teaching & Learning Company, Carthage, IL 62321-0010

Social Studies Experience
- Research where pumpkins are most plentiful and locate the places on a classroom map.

Music/Dramatic Experience
- Turn out the lights, put a flashlight in a jack-o'-lantern and read spooky stories by pumpkin light!

TLC10454 Copyright © Teaching & Learning Company, Carthage, IL 62321-0010

Great
Pumpkin

Great
Pumpkin

Great
Pumpkin

Great
Pumpkin

Physical/Sensory Experience

• Work together to turn a pumpkin into a jack-o'-lantern. After removing the pulp with an ice cream scoop, rinse the seeds off in a colander and save them to roast. Sprinkle nutmeg and cinnamon inside the pumpkin. When you light a candle inside, it will spread a wonderful aroma throughout your classroom. The candle, of course, should not be left burning without supervision.

Roasted Pumpkin Seeds

After rinsing the pulp off the seeds, mix them with melted butter and salt to taste. Garlic salt, celery salt and seasoning salt may also add an interesting taste. Bake for about 30 minutes at 300°F stirring occasionally.

• Play Pin the Nose on the Pumpkin (a variation of Pin the Tail on the Donkey). See reproducible on page 182.

TLC10454 Copyright © Teaching & Learning Company, Carthage, IL 62321-0010

Arts/Crafts Experience

• Have a pumpkin decorating contest. Provide paints and markers, dress-up items such as old jewelry and hats and other accessories. Give awards for the silliest, scariest, largest, smallest and most creative pumpkins.

• Let students cut out orange construction paper pumpkins, then add personality with facial features cut from magazines.

Extension Activities

• Visit a nearby pumpkin patch for a class field trip!

• Invite a farmer who grows pumpkins to come and talk to the class about growing and harvesting pumpkins.

Great
Pumpkin

Great
Pumpkin

Great
Pumpkin

Extension Activities continued

• Make homemade pumpkin bread, muffins or pumpkin cookies! Let students add candy corn and other candies to make jack-o'-lantern faces. For an easier treat, make instant pumpkin pudding and serve it with whipped cream.

• Follow the directions of your favorite brownie recipe, and bake the brownies in a round pizza pan. Frost it with orange frosting and add facial features with orange slice "eyebrows," candy eyes, mouth and nose and candy corn teeth.

Follow-Up/Homework Idea

• Serve dinner in a pumpkin or soup in small pumpkin bowls. Pumpkin-faced grilled cheese sandwiches will also add a festive flair! Simply carve a jack-o'-lantern face in the top slice of a rye bread grilled cheese sandwich.

TLC10454 Copyright © Teaching & Learning Company, Carthage, IL 62321-0010

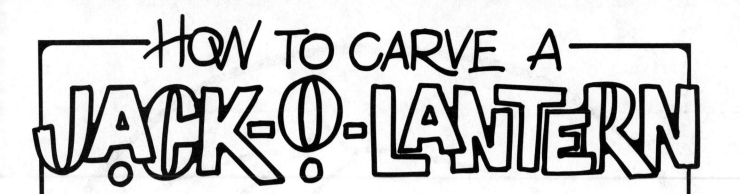

HOW TO CARVE A JACK-O-LANTERN

Name:_____

TLC10454 Copyright © Teaching & Learning Company, Carthage, IL 62321-0010

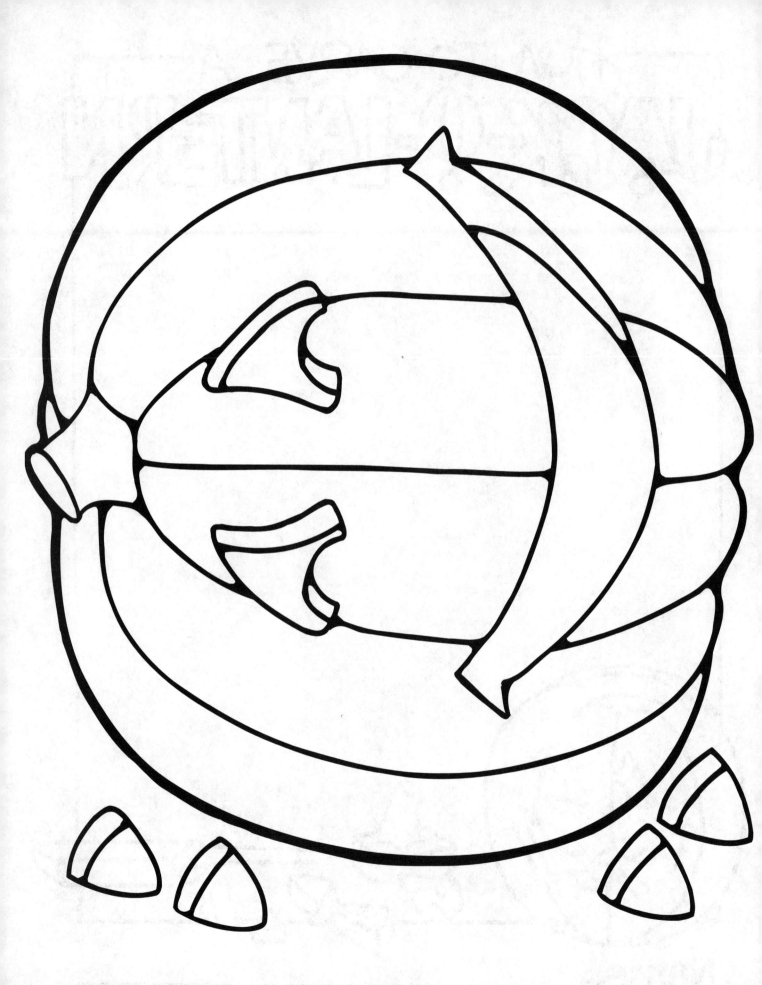

TLC10454 Copyright © Teaching & Learning Company, Carthage, IL 62321-0010

Halloween Hullabaloo Day

October 31

Setting the Stage

- Get some Halloween spirit in your room with helium-filled balloons with sheets thrown over them for ghosts, construction paper bats and spiders, and black and orange crepe paper streamers.

Historical Background

October 31st is generally observed as Halloween throughout the country.

Halloween
Hullabaloo

Halloween
Hullabaloo

Halloween
Hullabaloo

Literary Exploration

Arthur's Halloween by Marc Brown
The Best Halloween of All by Susan Wojciechowski
Boo! It's Halloween by Wendy Watson
By the Light of the Halloween Moon by Caroline Stutson
Cranberry Halloween by Wende Devlin
Froggy's Halloween by Jonathan London
Halloween by Gail Gibbons
Halloween by Miriam Nerlove
Halloween by Ron Reese
Halloween by Lucille Wood
Halloween ABC by Eve Merriam
Halloween Cookbook by Susan Purdy
Halloween Parade by Mary Lystad
The Halloween Party by John Lonzo Anderson
Halloween Party by Linda Shute
Halloween Poems by Myra Cohn Livingston
The Halloween Tree by Ray Bradbury
Haunted House by Jan Pienkowski
Hey-Ho for Halloween! by Lee Bennett Hopkins

TLC10454 Copyright © Teaching & Learning Company, Carthage, IL 62321-0010

Literary Exploration continued

In a Dark, Dark Room by Ruth Brown
It Hardly Seems Like Halloween by David Rose
It's Halloween by Jack Prelutsky
Miss Flora McFlimsey's Halloween by Mariana
My First Halloween by Tomie dePaola
Scary, Scary Halloween by Eve Bunting
That Terrible Halloween Night by James Stevenson
The Thirteen Days of Halloween by Carol Greene
Tom's Great Halloween Scare by John Peterson
Trick or Treat, Danny! by Edith Kunhardt
What Is Halloween? by Harriet Ziefert

Language Experience

• How many new words can your students make using the letters in *Halloween*?

Writing Experience

• Play spooky Halloween music while students write about visiting a haunted house, real or imaginary. See reproducible on page 190.

Science/Health Experience

- Review Halloween (nighttime) safety. Include light-colored outfits with adequate visibility and reflector tape on them, traveling with an adult, carrying a flashlight, staying in a familiar and lighted neighborhood. Have an adult inspect all Halloween treats, especially unwrapped items, discard anything suspicious or unknown.

- Do some of the classroom cooking experiences from Susan Purdy's *Halloween Cookbook*.

Music/Dramatic Experience

- Borrow Halloween music from a local library to set the mood in your classroom today.

- Check out the music from Ruth Roberts' *Halloween Songs to Tickle Your Funny Bone* from your local library.

TLC10454 Copyright © Teaching & Learning Company, Carthage, IL 62321-0010

Physical/Sensory Experience

• Play the old Halloween classic of Boris Karloff's, "The Monster Mash."

Arts/Crafts Experience

• Have students make a haunted house with flip-out windows and doors. After they color page 191, the doors and windows can be cut partly open with an X-acto™ knife (adult help will be needed). Then they can mount the page on construction paper. Students can draw scary creatures behind the doors and windows. See reproducible on page 191.

Name: _____

Extension Activities

- Set up a mini haunted house. Gather old refrigerator boxes for students to decorate and arrange. Add fun "body parts" to be touched: cold, cooked spaghetti for intestines, cooked cauliflower or cold cooked oatmeal for brains, grape eyeballs, candy corn teeth, rubber gloves filled with pudding and frozen for hands, raffia hair and prune ears. Students can crawl through the boxes and discover the scary items.

- Set up miniaturized "housing areas" around your room for trick-or-treating. Students can decorate trick or treat bags (with markers and stickers), then "knock" at each area to receive treats.

- Students can make Edible Jack-O'-Lantern Faces by adding olives and cheese or other pizza-type toppings to English muffins.

TLC10454 Copyright © Teaching & Learning Company, Carthage, IL 62321-0010

Extension Activities

• Here's a fun Halloween game! Place wrapped candy bars in the center of a game area. Students sit around the center and one person begins the game by rolling dice. Another pair of dice is started rolling from the opposite direction. Those getting doubles get to each pick a candy bar and hide it behind their backs. After the candy bars are all hidden behind student backs, each student tries to guess who has his or her favorite candy bar and tries to get it by rolling doubles. If the person guesses the name of the candy bar and who has it, he or she gets it.
If not, the game continues until the allotted playing time is over.

• Students enjoy traditional Halloween activities such as bobbing for apples, fishing for prizes in a cauldron or breaking a piñata. And, of course, Halloween wouldn't be complete without apple (juice) cider and doughnuts!

My visit to a **HAUNTED HOUSE**

Name _____

TLC10454 Copyright © Teaching & Learning Company, Carthage, IL 62321-001

Name: _____

TLC10454 Copyright © Teaching & Learning Company, Carthage, IL 62321-0010

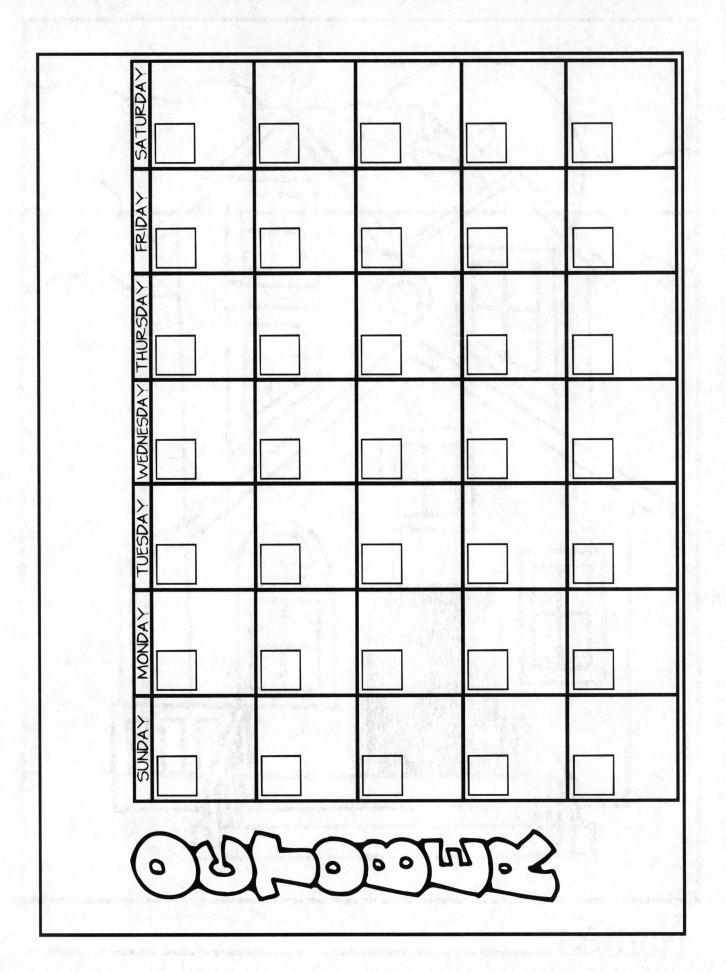

TLC10454 Copyright © Teaching & Learning Company, Carthage, IL 62321-0010